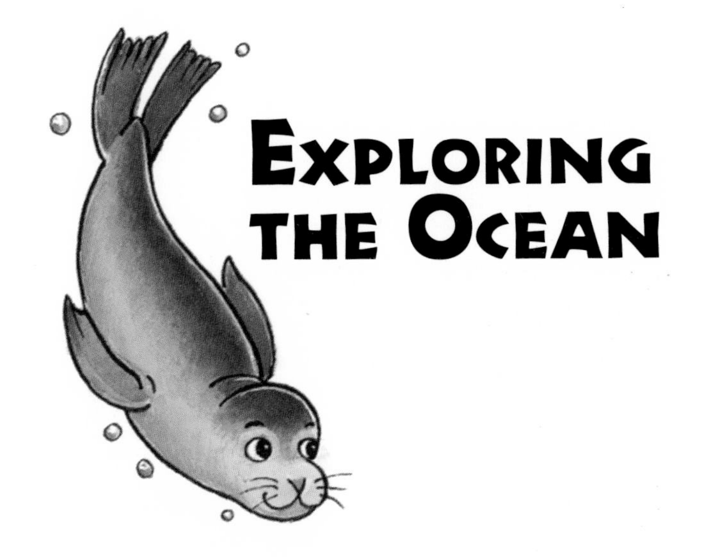
Exploring
the Ocean

EXPLORING THE OCEAN

A SUPPLEMENT TO CHILDCRAFT—THE HOW AND WHY LIBRARY

World Book, Inc.
a Scott Fetzer company
Chicago London Sydney Toronto

World Book, Inc.
525 W. Monroe
Chicago, IL 60661

ISBN 0-7166-0696-8
Library of Congress Catalog Card No. 65-25105
Printed in the United States of America

1 2 3 4 5 6 7 8 9 10 99 98 97 96

Contents

Preface 9

Ocean View 10-39

What is the ocean?
Jump right in
Wave makers
The ocean and weather
Sea Lab: Taming waves
The ocean's seesaw
Natural treasures
Be a sailor

Ocean Shores 40-75

What is the seashore?
Different shorescapes
Teeming tide pools
Wet and wriggly
Trees in the ocean?
Sea Lab: Make a seabed viewer
The shore underwater
Sea Challenge: School for otters
Birds of the seashore
Sea Lab: Sink or fly?

Shallow Ocean 76-107

What is the ocean's giant shelf?
Food for all
Beautiful building blocks
The coral reef community
Saving the reefs
Sea Challenge: Cucumbers in a pickle
Underwater forest
On your own
Sea Lab: Under pressure

Open Ocean 108-141

What is the open ocean?
At the surface
Sea Lab: Dating a fish
Record breakers
A long migration
Sea Challenge: Dolphins in peril
Life of a sand tiger shark
Entering the twilight zone
Ocean peaks

The Deep 142-167

What we know about the Deep
Dwellers of the Deep
Sea Lab: Make your own hot vent
"Gardens" in the dark
In the trenches
Sea Challenge: Braving the Deep
Secrets of the Titanic
Do you know the Deep?

POLAR OCEANS 168–201

The Cold Facts
Ice-ing on the Arctic cake
Animals of the Arctic
Life on the polynyas
Sea Lab: Create your own currents
Animals of the Antarctic
Birds of the polar regions
Too warm or not too warm?
Sea Challenge: A world laboratory

WORLD OCEAN 202–213

The ocean's system
Alien species on board
Will you help the ocean?

FIND OUT MORE 214

NEW WORDS 216

ILLUSTRATION ACKNOWLEDGMENTS 219

INDEX 220

STAFF

Publisher Emeritus
William H. Nault

President
John E. Frere

Vice President, Editor in Chief
Dick Dell

Vice President, Editorial Director
Michael Ross

Editorial

Managing Editor
Maureen Mostyn Liebenson

Associate Editor
Sharon Nowakowski

Permissions Editor
Janet T. Peterson

Contributing Editor
Diana K. Myers

Copy Editor
Irene B. Keller

Writers
Daniel J. Barnekow
Pamela Bliss
Mary Feely
Ellen Hughes
Kathleen E. Kain
Lisa A. Klobuchar
Anne M. O'Malley

Indexer
David Pofelski

Director of Research
Mary Norton

Researchers
Lynn Durbin
Cheryl Graham
Sally Halderman
Karen McCormack
Loranne Shields
Kristina Vaicikonis

Contributing Researcher
Rita Vander Meulen

Consultants
Mia Tegner, Ph.D.
Research Marine Biologist
Scripps Institution of Oceanography
University of California, San Diego
La Jolla, California

Bert Vescolani, B.S.Ed.
Curator of Education
John G. Shedd Aquarium
Chicago, Illinois

Art

Executive Director
Roberta Dimmer

Art Director
Wilma Stevens

Designers
Donna Cook
Design 5

Contributing Artists
Carol Brozman
Mary-Ann Lupa
Valerie Nelson-Metlay
Sandy Newell
Lucy Smith

Electronic Production Artists
Sarah Figlio
Lucy Smith

Senior Photographs Editor
Sandra Dyrlund

Photographs Editor
Carol Parden

Product Production

Vice President, Production and Technology
Daniel N. Bach

Director, Manufacturing/ Pre-Press
Sandra Van den Broucke

Manufacturing Manager
Barbara Podczerwinski

Production Manager
Joann Seastrom

Proofreaders
Anne Dillon
Karen Lenburg

PREFACE

You may be familiar with stories of mermaids and pirates, but life in and around the big blue can be just as exciting as any make-believe tale. In this book, you'll learn all about the ocean's real treasures, which include sand tiger sharks, marine explorers, a school for otters, and real alien species.

With the help of a different friendly tour guide in each chapter, you'll discover the ocean's giant seesaw, find out what kinds of worms live on the sea floor, explore an ocean forest, learn about farms at sea, and visit an oasis in the Arctic.

You'll also have fun playing ocean games, doing "Sea Labs"—experiments that you can do alone or with a friend—and reading "Sea Challenges," which explain how people and the ocean affect each other.

After diving into this book, you'll feel like you've explored the ocean blue—even if you've never actually been to the shore.

OCEAN VIEW

Ahoy, there! I'm Maggie Waters—at your service. I can explain the wet suit. I'm an oceanographer. I spend my time exploring the ocean and studying all its secrets. And of course, I'm as happy as (what else?) a clam! Are you ready for a wet, wild, and wonderful tour?

WHAT IS THE OCEAN?

It's a world of surprises! See for yourself!

Where is it? Almost everywhere! More than 70 percent of Earth's surface is covered by the ocean. That's about 140 million square miles (362 million square kilometers) of the planet's surface underwater. Gulp!

We call different parts of the ocean by different names: the Atlantic, the Pacific, the Arctic, the Antarctic, and the Indian oceans. But they are all part of one vast world ocean.

How deep is the ocean? On average, the ocean floor is about 2 1/2 miles (4 kilometers) below the surface. It's a distance equal to about 2,750 10-year-olds lined up head to toe.

Talk about salty! Ocean water is about 3.5 percent salt on average—though some areas are much saltier than others. If the world ocean suddenly dried up, it would leave an enormous pile of salt—a pile big enough to make a new continent the size of Africa!

How cool! The ocean's water temperatures vary, depending on the part of the ocean and the depth.

In the polar regions, the surface water freezes.

Near the sun-baked equator, you could say it's hot, with surface temperatures reaching about 86 °F (30 °C).

Have you ever had your ears "pop" or had trouble breathing as you went up in an airplane or an elevator in a tall building? If so, that's because your ears and lungs were adjusting to the change in air pressure. When you go down in the ocean, your ears and lungs will also feel different as they adjust to the change in water and air pressure.

Whose ocean is it? Until recently, the waters controlled by an individual country extended only 3 miles (4.8 kilometers)—the distance a cannonball could be shot from shore. Today, most countries have territorial rights over the first 12 nautical miles (22 kilometers) of ocean off their shores—a nautical mile is slightly longer than a land mile.

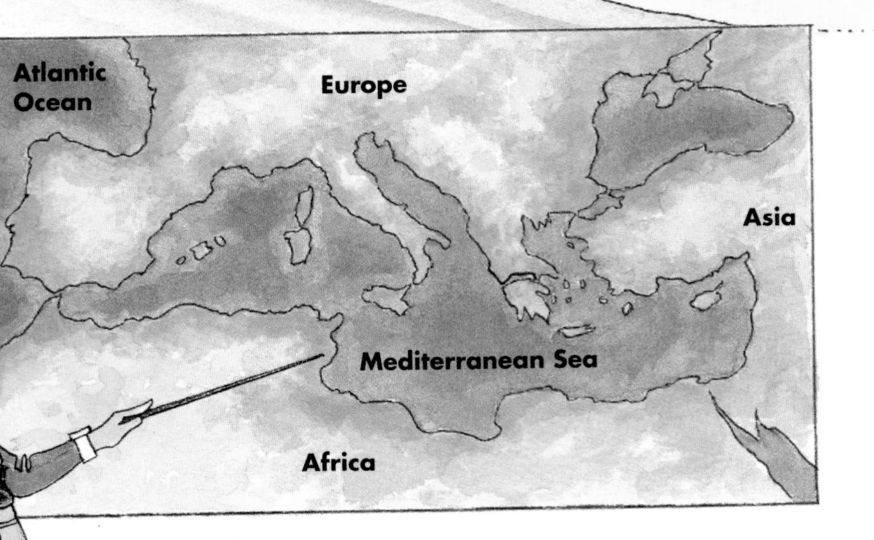

Do you say *sea*? Actually, a sea is a body of salt water that is closed off from the ocean, like the Dead Sea, or partly closed off, like the Mediterranean. But it's okay to call the ocean the *sea*. Most people do from time to time.

JUMP RIGHT IN!

Let me show you around the ocean, my favorite place. Almost anything you find on land is also found in the ocean, and is sometimes bigger.

You want mountains? There are plenty of them. And there are canyons that are so big that they make the Grand Canyon seem puny.

Looking around the edges of the continents, you can see a gently sloping rim under the water. That's the ocean's continental shelf.

Barnacle Bit

Vacation with a fish? You bet you can at Jules's Undersea Lodge, off the coast of Key Largo, Florida. It's the world's first undersea hotel. Guests suit up to swim down 30 feet (9 meters), taking their luggage along in waterproof containers.

At the edge of the shelf, there's a steep drop until you're on the vast ocean floor. The ocean floor is nearly as mysterious as the surface of the moon. But with high-tech equipment, scientists have been learning more and more about what goes on down there.

Now let's head for shore. But which kind? Rocky, muddy, or sandy? You can see so much life clinging to rocky shores. And if you time it right, you can see green sea turtles lay their eggs on Costa Rica's sandy northwest beaches.

In the shallow waters you can find such natural wonders as Australia's Great Barrier Reef. This huge, beautiful reef serves as home to an incredible variety of strange and colorful sea creatures.

Out past the shallow waters is the open ocean. Out there, sea birds hover and then dive in for a quick meal. Animals from deeper waters also come up to the surface to dine. You might even see dolphins playing out in the open ocean.

Down below the open ocean are the watery depths. The only light that far down is blue—and some of it comes from the fish! The creatures of the deep are kind of weird, even to an oceanographer.

DOLPHINS

HOT VENTS

Yes, it's pretty cold down there, but some creatures down deep live near hot vents. The water shooting out of a vent is really cooking. It's heated by all that molten rock below the earth's crust.

If that's too hot for you, then let's look at the North Pole. It's a cold place, but the polar bears there are pretty comfortable. The South Pole is also cold. It's on the Antarctic icecap, the ocean's icebox. But if all that ice melted at once, we wouldn't just have a puddle. The sea would rise 200 feet (61 meters) all over the world!

Under the ice are giant sea spiders. And they're not the only strange creatures that live in this icy brew. There are also krill, seals, penguins, and whales.

There's so much for you to see. Read on!

WAVE MAKERS

Grab your surfboards! I'll have you talking crests, troughs, bores, and tsunamis in no time.

You already know that wind causes most ocean waves, and the faster the wind and the longer it blows, the bigger the waves it'll make. But there's more.

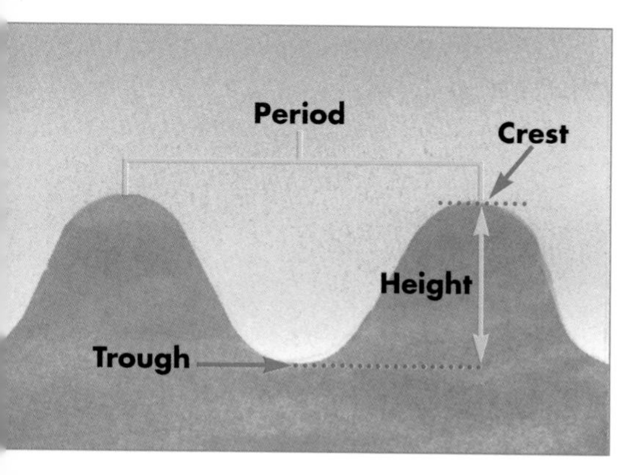

Looking for the biggest wave? The height of a wave is measured from its *crest* to its *trough.* The crest is the wave's highest part or peak. The trough is the lowest part, in the depression the wave makes in the water's surface. In a severe storm, waves 30 to 50 feet (9 to 15 meters) high are common. The biggest wave ever recorded on the open ocean was 112 feet (34 meters) high.

Barnacle Bit

Don't change your watch yet, but the friction of the tides is actually slowing the rotation of the earth. Billions of years ago, a day was about four hours long. In the very distant future, a day will be 50 times longer than it is now.

The time between one crest and the next is a wave's *period*. Once a wave is created, its period never changes until it runs out of energy or hits a beach.

Watch some waves and learn. Are they the same distance apart, the same size, and coming from the same direction? Then they were probably born in a storm over the open ocean, maybe thousands of miles away. Or are the waves different sizes and shapes, and coming in on top of one another at an uneven pace? These were probably created by local winds or passing boats.

Let's not forget about waves created by the tides. On a Mediterranean shore, sunbathers laze as the tide slips softly up the beach. But in Canada's Bay of Fundy, all seagoing traffic stops while the tide rushes in, raising the water level more than 50 feet (15 meters). Why the difference? The shape of the sea floor and shore. A broad, gently sloping beach lets the tide rise slowly. But when a steep ocean slope squeezes the same amount of energy into a narrow bay or inlet, the incoming water has nowhere to go but up! The tide rushes in as one big *bore*, a high wall of churning water.

Perhaps the most dangerous waves are *tsunamis* (tsoo NAH meez). A tsunami may be

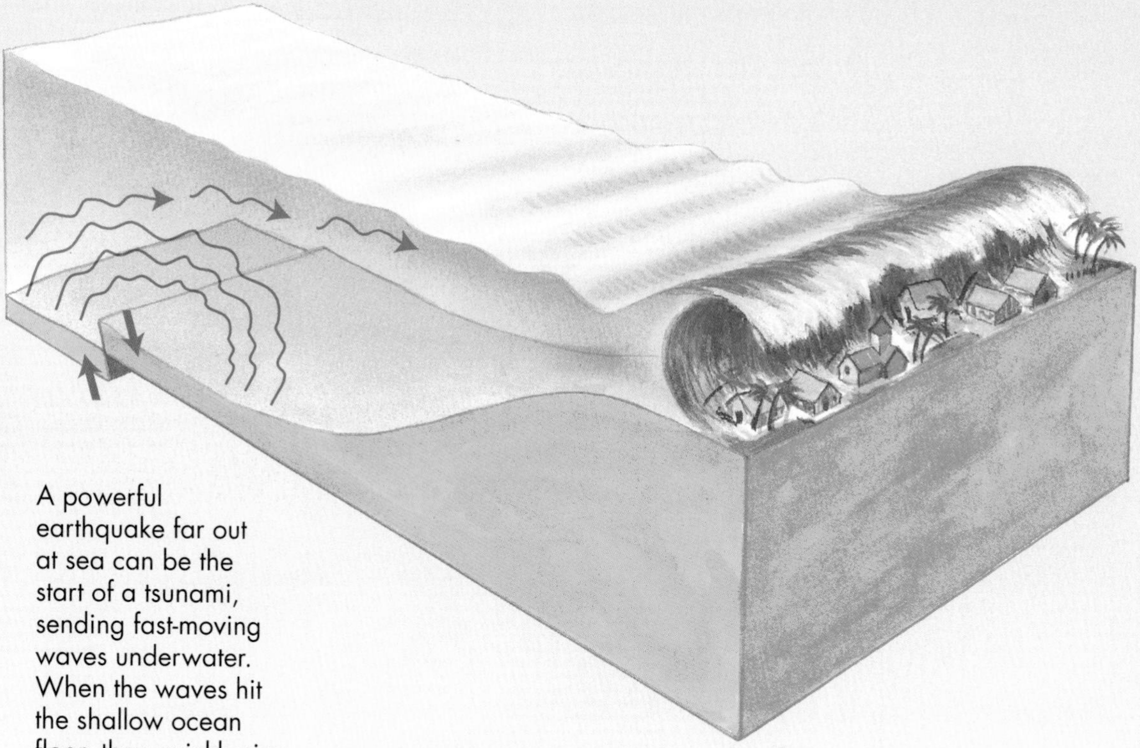

A powerful earthquake far out at sea can be the start of a tsunami, sending fast-moving waves underwater. When the waves hit the shallow ocean floor, they quickly rise up, and then crash down on the seaside.

created when an undersea earthquake or violent storm at sea sends a powerful shock wave through the water. Tsunamis move as fast as 500 to 600 miles (800 to 970 kilometers) per hour beneath the surface of the open ocean. In deep water, one could pass under your boat and you wouldn't feel a thing! But look out when a tsunami nears the shore. The shallow waters force it to slow way down—to 30 to 100 miles (48 to 161 kilometers) per hour—causing the wave to suddenly rise up and then slam down on the land. Such huge waves have wiped out seaside villages.

Water Word

A *wave train* is a group of powerful swells (big, smooth waves) traveling together across the open ocean. When one wave train collides with another, the crash may create monster-sized waves that can break ships apart!

Wait! Waves aren't all bad. Water that is splashed and pushed about gets restocked with oxygen and helps distribute food—all of which helps support marine life. In addition, waves toss all sorts of ocean treats onto the shore, serving hungry land creatures.

This gull is feeding on a meal washed up by the waves—a small dogfish shark.

THE OCEAN AND WEATHER

Care to join me in a glass of 3-billion-year-old water? That's right, it's 3 billion years old—and as fresh as any water on earth!

You see, almost every drop of water on earth today has been here since the world began. It's the same water the dinosaurs swam in, and it's the same water the Vikings sailed. Our water is constantly being recycled by the ocean and nature's *water cycle*. The sun shines down, causing water to evaporate from the ocean, as well as from rivers, plants, and more. As vapor, the water rises into the sky, gathers into clouds,

and eventually returns to the earth, usually as rain or snow. The water gathers in streams and rivers, and mostly in the ocean. Then the water begins the whole cycle again.

The ocean and the water cycle play a large role in our weather. The ocean helps keep our weather comfortable. By absorbing the sun's heat in the summer and releasing it all winter long, the ocean keeps temperatures on earth from getting horribly HOT or terribly c-c-cold.

So why is the weather always changing and sometimes difficult to predict? Partly because the air above the ocean and the waters in the ocean move around. Wind over the open

The water you drink and bathe with today has been recycled and reused countless times over billions of years.

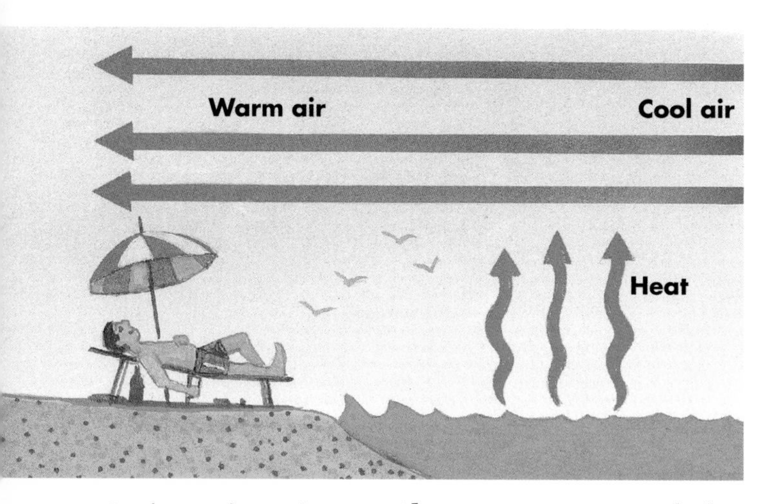

Cool air is heated as it passes over warm water.

ocean not only creates waves, but it also helps create *currents.* Ocean currents are similar to powerful rivers. As they circulate, currents move warm and cold waters to different areas. As they move, they warm or cool the air above and affect weather conditions worldwide.

In some areas, *upwelling* occurs when the winds cause surface waters near the coast to move offshore. Colder, deeper waters, into which many nutrients have sunk, then rise to the surface to replace the lost water. Upwelling brings nutritious waters from the deep up to the surface, providing food for many marine organisms.

The Gulf Stream is a major ocean current that starts in the Caribbean near the equator. The sun-warmed current moves up from the equator, around the end of Florida, and up along the coast, bringing warm waters to the southeastern shores of the United States. At about Cape Hatteras, North Carolina, the current leaves the shore, but it travels near the coast until about Long Island. Then it heads mostly east, across the Atlantic to the coasts of Great Britain and western Europe.

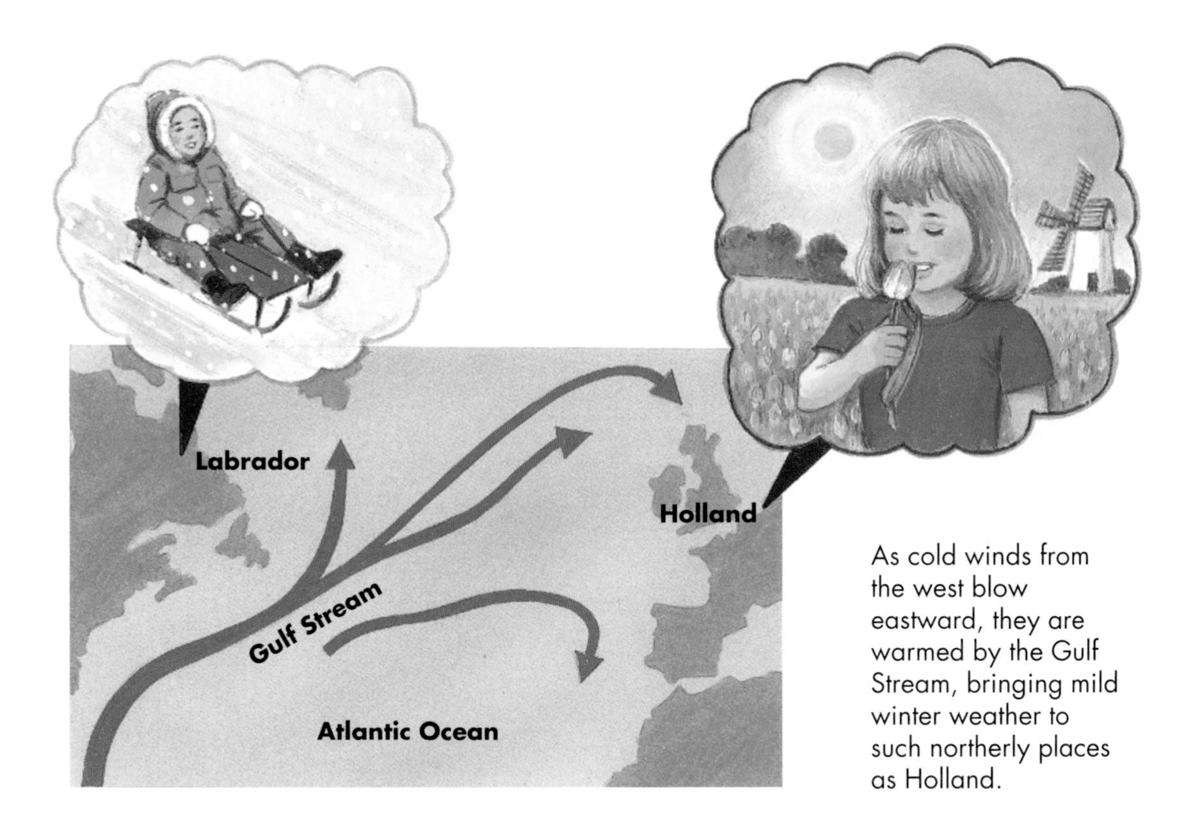

As cold winds from the west blow eastward, they are warmed by the Gulf Stream, bringing mild winter weather to such northerly places as Holland.

In winter, the temperature of the current east of Cape Hatteras is warmer than the air temperature, so the water warms the air. The winds that blow eastward toward Europe are warmed as they cross the Gulf Stream. The British Isles and Norway, which are as close to the North Pole as icy Labrador, enjoy milder winters because the warm air blows over their coasts. Holland's tulips, France's vineyards, and Sweden's green pastures all bloom in the warm weather brought by the Gulf Stream.

Barnacle Bit

For nearly 400 years, Spanish treasure hunters traveled in the Gulf Stream current. Many of their ships were wrecked by hurricanes and rocky shores. Modern treasure hunters think that about one-eighth of that Spanish treasure still lies on the ocean floor below the Gulf Stream.

Barnacle Bit

Scientists can often learn from things that happen outside of a laboratory, even from human mishaps. In 1992, a container fell off a ship, and 29,000 plastic bath toys—brightly colored ducks, frogs, turtles, and beavers—floated away on the currents of the Pacific Ocean. Using computers and information about where some of the toys reached land, some scientists who study currents are testing their ability to predict ocean flow. The first little fellows came ashore in Alaska. Others are expected to ride currents into the North Atlantic, eventually washing up in Iceland, Norway, and the United Kingdom.

Currents that move from the poles toward the equator tend to be cool. The Humboldt Current flows north along the west coast of South America. Penguins typically live in the Antarctic, but they sometimes follow the cool current as far north as the equator. The cold Benguela Current cools the air and water along the southwest coast of Africa, while the warm Kuroshio current flows east across the Pacific from Japan. These currents join up, break apart, and flow above and below each other.

SEA LAB

Taming Waves

Here's your chance to play Mother Nature while you take a close-up look at wave energy and rain.

Things you need:

- ***a bathtub with a shower head***
- ***a towel for the scientist***

1. Fill the bathtub half full with cold water—be sure to tell an adult first. Let the water surface become smooth.

2. Using your outstretched arm, sweep the water toward the end of the tub that has the shower head, starting a strong wave. Be careful not to slosh water out of the tub.

3. While the wave is in full swing, turn on the shower, pointing the spray onto the center of the tub. What happens to the wave when your "rain" hits it? Make another wave. This time don't turn on the shower and see the difference.

Scientists have found that harmless little raindrops can tame a wild and stormy sea. Lots of tiny raindrops splashing into a choppy sea break up the organized energy of the waves. The rain stirs the water, and stirring the water destroys the waves.

THE OCEAN'S SEESAW

Scientists have been studying a curious phenomenon called El Niño, which affects weather in and out of the ocean worldwide. El Niño is part of the ENSO (El Niño/Southern Oscillation) cycle. It's a complex cycle, but it's easy to understand if you compare it to a seesaw. An *oscillation* (AHS uh LAY shuhn) is a kind of regular, up-and-down change. A layer of water called the *thermocline* separates the warm surface waters from the waters of the colder depths. During the ENSO cycle, the thermocline sways slowly up and down, like a giant seesaw, in the western and eastern Pacific. Let me show you.

WATER WORD

La Niña, which means "little girl" in Spanish, is the opposite of El Niño. La Niña cools down the ocean's surface temperatures. When that happens, Australia gets more rain; Peru gets drier and cooler; and India, Burma, and Thailand go on typhoon alert.

Ordinarily, mighty winds sweep west from South America across the Pacific Ocean along the equator. These winds push the warm surface water to the western Pacific and Indian oceans. As the water moves west, the thermocline rises toward the surface in the eastern Pacific, allowing deep, cold water to rise up and replace the warm water. In this phase, warm weather and torrential rains hit much of India and Southeast Asia.

But when the strong winds weaken, the seesaw begins to tilt the other way—to the El Niño phase. Without the strong wind, the westward currents weaken and the warm surface waters begin to move east, bringing clouds and rain with them. In addition, the thermocline in the eastern Pacific deepens and prevents deep, cold water from rising to the surface. The water that warmed the air in the

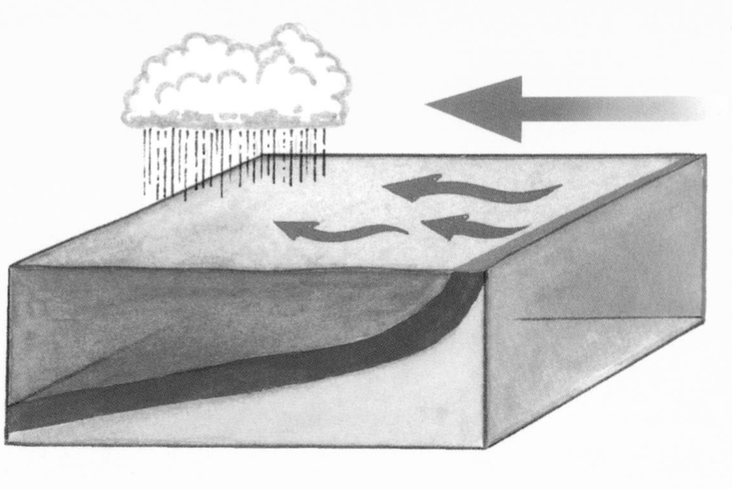

Typically, strong winds push warm surface waters westward across the Pacific. The thermocline begins to tilt as cool waters from the deep rise to replace the lost surface water.

During El Niño, the strong winds weaken or stop, and the ocean's seesaw begins to tilt the other way, bringing warm water and rain to the east.

west now warms air in the east, affecting wind patterns and weather worldwide.

Scientists do not fully understand what makes the thermocline seesaw. They do not know why the winds weaken, for instance. But they do know that the effects of the El Niño phase can be disastrous. Fishing crews along the coast of Peru generally haul in some of the world's greatest catches, because the cold water that wells up along the coast brings nutrients to feed large numbers of fish. But when El Niño lets the warm surface waters roll in, the cold water—and its food supply—sinks down. And, as the food disappears, so do the fish and birds.

In the United States, typically sunny California is drenched with rain during El Niño. In upstate New York, midwinter warm spells bring hibernating bears out of their caves. In western Africa, the corn crop is destroyed by sudden droughts. Australia, the Philippines, Mexico, and India go without rain while typhoons and heavy rains pound Tahiti and Hawaii.

Usually, El Niño arrives every few years around Christmas, and leaves before the year is up. But sometimes it stays for years, making it difficult for people to cope with its effects.

El Niño brings heavy rains and flooding to parts of the United States, like this section of Los Angeles.

NATURAL TREASURES

The ocean is filled with riches—not just gold that pirates lost, but also resources that can be used for food, medicines, farming, energy, and more.

Feeling hungry? Have some kombu. Do you want yours fresh, in soup, stewed, dried, pickled, salted, sweetened, shredded, or in candy? In Asia, this kelp, or seaweed, is enjoyed in all these ways. In fact, all algae are rich in vitamins and minerals.

The sea offers terrific farming and ranching possibilities. People in Asia have farmed fish for centuries, and now the industry, known as *aquaculture*, is catching on everywhere. Oyster farms flourish off the coasts of Australia, New Zealand, and Spain; kelp and algae farms in

Offshore pens hold salmon being raised for market on a New Zealand fish farm.

Japan, the Philippines and the United States; salmon ranches in Canada, New Zealand, Norway, and Scotland—and I'm just fishing the surface here!

The ocean is a medicine chest, too. We get antibiotics from sea sponges and seaweeds, heart medicine from sea anemones, and a wound-healing "band-aid" material for eye surgery from mussels. And there's more help on the way. Fish toxins, clam

Barnacle Bit

Roman naturalist Pliny (A.D. 23 or 24-79) saw the potential healing power of sea plants. In his writing, Pliny discussed possible medicines from the sea that are only now being fully researched.

livers, and *chitin* (KY tihn), a tough material in the shells of certain marine animals, are being studied for their use in making new medicines.

Underwater mining is really just getting underway, but every mineral found on dry land is also found in or under the ocean. Seawater contains arsenic, gold, iodine, lead, silver, uranium, zinc, and, of course, salt. Sand and gravel, iron, sulfur, and coal are all mined from the sea floor. Manganese nodules are scattered over the sea floor. These clumps contain valuable resources, such as manganese, copper, nickel, and cobalt. But working underwater can be complicated, so mining the ocean is often more

At high tide, ocean water flowing into the mouth of the Rance River is trapped behind this dam. As it flows out again, it drives generators that produce electricity.

expensive than mining on land. Scientists are looking for less expensive ways to get minerals from the sea.

Huge oil rigs in the North Sea, the Gulf of Mexico, the Persian Gulf, off northern Australia, off California, and in the Arctic Ocean are reaching vast supplies of oil and gas below the ocean floor. And don't forget those powerful tides and currents. People use them for energy too. At the mouth of the narrow Rance River in France, the powerful tide is caught behind a dam and then released to make electricity!

Ocean Thermal Energy Conversion, or OTEC, is another plan for ocean power. *Thermal* means "heat." OTEC uses the temperature difference between warm surface water and cold water pumped from the deep to create energy.

Things you need:

- *two pencils*
- *a travel log or piece of paper for each sailor*
- *a die*
- *two place markers*
- *another sailor*

Travel the sea with a friend. Determine who will set sail first. Then take turns rolling the die and following the instructions at sea. Use your travel log to keep track of your points. The one with the most at the end wins. Bon voyage! (That's French for "Have a good trip!")

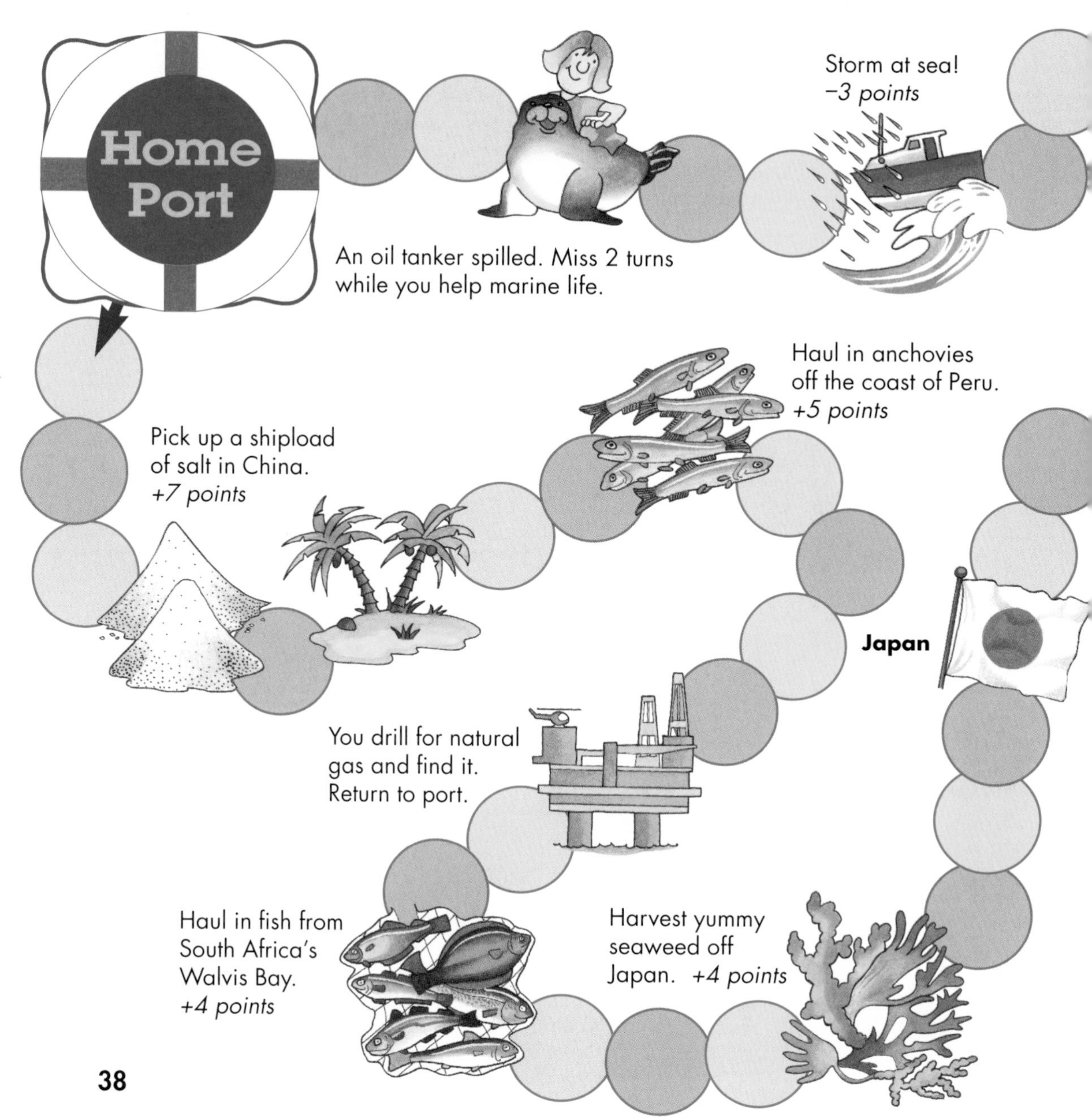

Catch the Gulf Stream and ride free to Holland.
Holland
Scotland
Listen, tidal bore coming— miss 1 turn.
El Niño's back— lose your anchovy catch and 1 turn. –4 points
Load a tanker with oil from a drilling rig in the North Sea off the coast of Scotland. +4 points
Here comes a wave train. Hop on a swell and ride to the nearest island. +3 points
Stop to collect shrimp in your new shrimp farm in Ecuador. +8 points
Tsunami! Drop your Japanese seaweed and go back 3 spaces. –4 points
France
Your oyster farm in South Korea is booming. +10 points
Ride the tide and collect electric power in France. +7 points
Catch 3 loads full of cod from the Grand Banks. +3 points

OCEAN SHORES

Howdy! My name is Hermit Crab. Forgive me for not shaking hands. I can tell you all there is to know about shores, because hermit crabs live on shores all over the world. And on shores where we don't live, you'll find our crabby relatives! Turn the page and see.

WHAT IS THE SEASHORE?

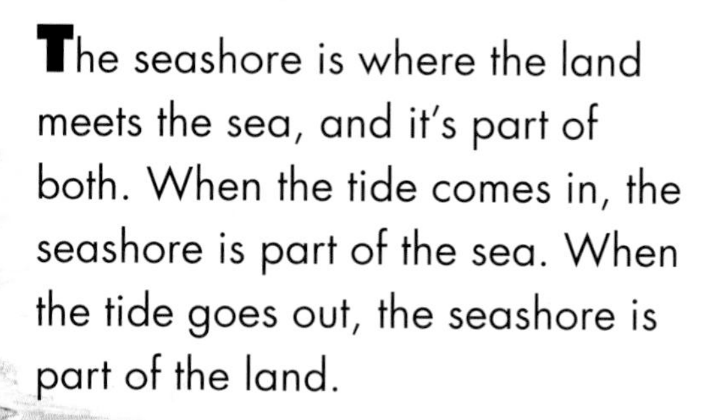

The seashore is where the land meets the sea, and it's part of both. When the tide comes in, the seashore is part of the sea. When the tide goes out, the seashore is part of the land.

Tides are created by the gravitational pull of the sun and moon on the earth. Gravity pulls the ocean water, making it bulge toward the sun and moon. Sometimes you can see the effects of the bulge along the seashore, where the water level rises and falls approximately every twelve hours.

In addition to the tides, the wind, currents, and waves also shape the seashore and its community. For example, over time, wind, waves, and currents can move the sand on a beach out to sea or farther along a coast.

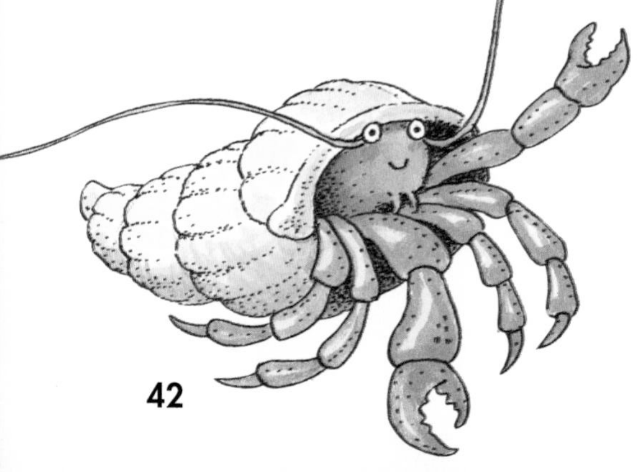

Many seashores act as nurseries, supplying young animals with food and protecting them until they are strong enough to go out to sea.

The seashore is where rivers eventually meet the ocean. Rivers carry *sediment* (SEHD uh muhnt)—which includes sand, dirt, and waste—into the coastal waters and the homes of marine animals. Currents, waves, and tides carry some of the sediment to the open ocean.

Many animals that spend their entire life on the beach don't even move—they just wait for the waves or the tide to bring them food.

Different kinds of living things make their homes on different parts of the seashore. Some live above the level of the highest tides, where the ocean never reaches. Others live below the low tide line, where they are always underwater. Still others live in the in-between areas where the tide comes and goes.

DIFFERENT SHORESCAPES

There are three main kinds of seashore—rocky, sandy, and muddy. A rocky shore has more life than any other, so let's scuttle along and have a look.

Anything that lives on a rocky shore faces two challenges. It must cling to the rocks for dear life as the waves of the sea wash over it. And it must stay moist when the tide is out.

Large seaweeds called kelp live in areas below the tide. They grab onto the rocks with long, fingerlike *holdfasts*. Some other seaweeds can survive drying out. Take channel wrack. It's black and brittle when it's dry, but it's like new when the tide comes in.

Many mollusks live on rocky shores. Mollusks are soft animals with no bones. Most have hard shells and can anchor themselves to

Some seaweeds can stay dry and survive between high tides. Rockweed thrives in and out of water on this Maine shore.

the rocks. The limpet has a foot that grips a rock with suction and a coating of mucus. Its saucer-shaped shell lessens the force of waves and protects it from crabs and seabirds.

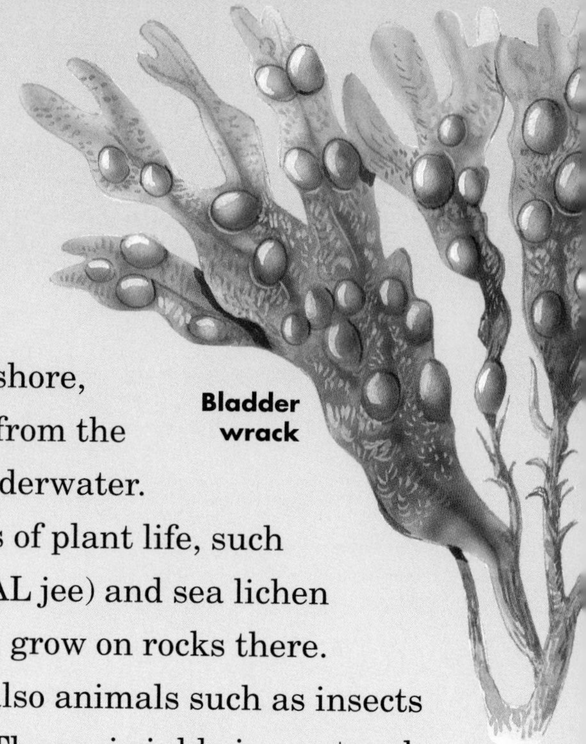

Along a rocky shore, the area farthest from the sea is rarely underwater. Simple forms of plant life, such as algae (AL jee) and sea lichen (LY kuhn), grow on rocks there. There are also animals such as insects and periwinkles. The periwinkle is one tough sea snail. To avoid drying out, it closes a kind of trapdoor on its shell. While its shell is shut, the periwinkle stops breathing—temporarily.

A little closer to the water, the shore is covered by the sea part of the time. There you can see many small seaweeds. One, the spiral wrack, has a short, broad *frond* (leaflike area). And there are lovely limpets and other shelled animals. Barnacles are shrimplike animals that attach to rocks and build a hard case around themselves.

Are you ready for some real action? Follow me, friend. Life abounds where the shore is

Bladder wrack

Limpet

Periwinkle

covered by water most of the time. Large seaweeds called bladder wrack provide food and shelter for many animals. Here you can also find coralline—bright pink algae encased in lime—along with spiky purple sea urchins, colorful sea stars (starfish), and vibrant sponges. Tube worms glue grains of sand together to make tubes, which they use to attach themselves to rocks.

I see members of my family everywhere. Shore crabs roam the shore seeking food—dead or alive! Sometimes pea crabs like to snuggle inside a clam's shell and steal food that the clam collects.

Compared with rocky shores, sandy shores are like ghost towns, because plants, animals,

Wind, waves, and sun make sandy shores fun for people but hard for plants and animals to live on.

and other living things can't cling to loose sand the way they can to rocks. Animals bury themselves in the sand for protection from waves and the drying rays of the sun.

As the razor clam lies in the sand, it uses its long foot as an anchor. Razor clams can feel the slightest vibrations. If they feel us approaching, they'll rapidly dig deeper.

Muddy shores develop where rivers enter the sea, mixing salt water and fresh water. One such shore is the salt marsh. Plants that can adjust to this mixture provide shelter and nutrients for many organisms. Several kinds of grasses, especially cordgrass, thrive in salt marshes. As cordgrass absorbs water through its roots, it filters out salt. If any salt slips in, the cordgrass *excretes* (gets rid of) it through special pores on its leaves. Other salt marsh plants include the sea blite, sea lavender, and glasswort.

Razor clam

Barnacle Bit

Some tropical seeds may travel thousands of miles—sometimes for years—on the open ocean before finding a home. A coconut, one of the larger seeds, can float 3,000 miles (4,830 kilometers), hit land, and start growing into a tree.

Salt marshes support many kinds of plant and animal life. This one, in Spain, is home to flocks of flamingos and many smaller shore birds.

The sea animals in a salt marsh attract wading birds, such as the bittern. This bird uses its striped markings for protection. When danger approaches, the bittern points its bill upward and stands still so that its stripes blend with the cordgrass. If the grass sways in the breeze, the bittern sways right along with it.

Raccoons and muskrats visit salt marshes to dine on crabs. Owls and hawks come here to hunt the small animals. And in subtropical regions, alligators prowl, hoping to make a meal of all kinds of visitors.

TEEMING TIDE POOLS

When the tide goes out from a rocky shore, some water remains in pools among the rocks. In areas that are not too hot or cold, tide pools are like tiny seas, crowded with animals and life. Let's check one out.

Many tide pools are decorated with creatures that look like colorful flowers—sea anemones. Each "flower" is actually an animal clinging to a rock with its built-in suction cup. The sea anemone's "petals" are tentacles filled with poisonous, stinging cells. The poison paralyzes the anemone's prey, which is then swept into its mouth.

Most animals avoid the sea anemone, but I sometimes carry one around on my shell. There it can sweep up all the food it wants. In return, its poisonous stings protect me from octopuses and other enemies. Some tide pool residents are even tougher than the sea anemone. One such creature is the sea spider—no relation to land spiders. Most sea

Goose barnacles, sea stars, and sea anemones cling to the rocky rim of this tide pool in Olympic National Park, Washington.

Star-eyed hermit crab

spiders that live near the shore are only about 1/2 inch (1.2 centimeters) long. But they eat sea anemones by boring into their bodies with a fanglike proboscis (proh BAHS ihs). Scientists think the sea spider's tough outer covering may protect it from the sea anemone's stinging cells.

Another tide pool toughie is the nudibranch (NOO duh brangk), a colorful slug. Because it has no shell, the nudibranch looks like an easy target. But that's not so! Its favorite nibble is a sea anemone's tentacles. After the meal, the sea anemone's poisonous cells move into spiny cerata, which line the nudibranch's back. Then the nudibranch uses them to defend itself.

You'll also find lots of my crabby cousins in any

These nudibranchs are armed. The colorful fringe that covers them is filled with stinging cells from the sea anemones they eat.

tide pool. One is the porcelain crab. Its flat body allows the porcelain crab to squirm under a slab of rock to hide from predators.

A whelk opens a clam shell to feed on the meat inside.

Many tide pools are lined with mussels, a kind of shellfish. Mussels like company—as many as 160,000 of them may crowd into 11 square feet (1 square meter).

Mussels anchor themselves to rocks by spinning long, silky threads called byssal threads. When these threads harden, they glue the mussel to the rock.

The mussel's shell protects it from many enemies, but not from the whelk. This meat-eating snail is just crazy about mussel. Whelks use their raspy mouths to drill into a mussel's shell. Some kinds of whelks also dribble an acid that melts a hole in the shell. And once the whelk makes an opening, it's all over for the mussel.

Barnacle Bit

Long ago, the byssal threads of the fan mussel were woven into golden cloth for Europe's kings and queens.

Some fish are at home in tide pools, but others sometimes get trapped in them. Certain gobies have an amazing ability. When these gobies sense danger, they leap to a different tide pool. How do they know exactly where the next tide pool is? That's a mystery.

WET AND WRIGGLY

When the tide is out, a sandy beach may seem deserted—no signs of life at all. But just below the surface, the sand is full of life—wet and wriggly life! Worms burrow in the sand to avoid being dried up by the sun or swept out to sea by the waves.

To move through its world of heavy sand, a sea worm uses its head and changes its shape.

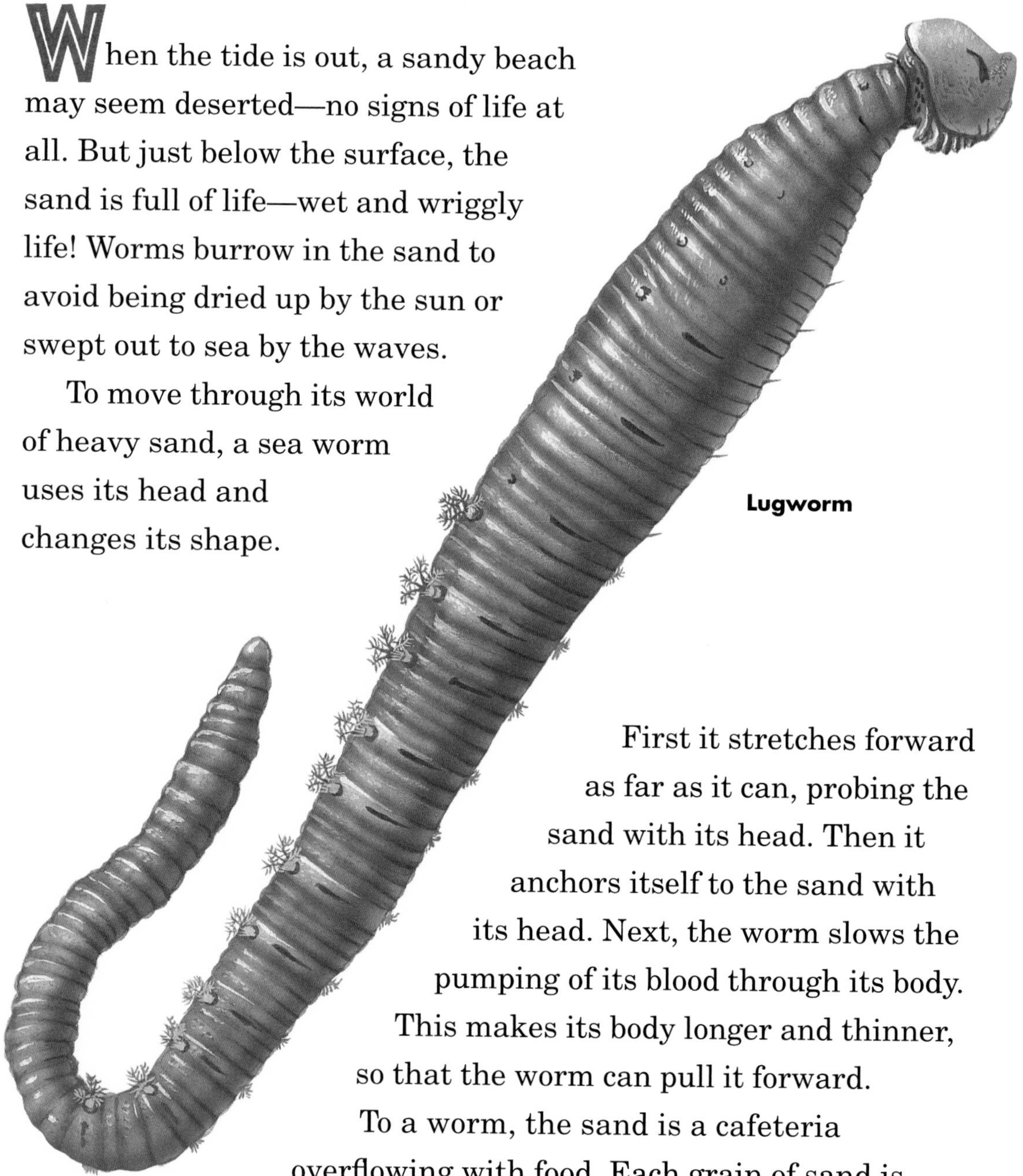

Lugworm

First it stretches forward as far as it can, probing the sand with its head. Then it anchors itself to the sand with its head. Next, the worm slows the pumping of its blood through its body. This makes its body longer and thinner, so that the worm can pull it forward.

To a worm, the sand is a cafeteria overflowing with food. Each grain of sand is surrounded by a thin film of water stocked with all kinds of goodies—tiny shrimplike creatures,

water mites, and other microscopic organisms, such as algae.

The greediest of all sea worms is probably the lugworm, or lobworm, which is 5 to 8 inches (13 to 20 centimeters) long. The lugworm isn't a fussy eater—it devours everything in front of it. It swallows huge mouthfuls of sand, digests any food, and excretes the rest in a worm-shaped casting. If you look on the beach when the tide is out, you're likely to see these castings.

All day long, the lugworm lies in a U-shaped tunnel under the sand, relying on the sea to bring food to the mouth of its tunnel. It paddles with its fanlike "feet" to pull in water and food.

A lugworm lies in an underground tunnel, taking in food from the sea at one end and putting out castings at the other.

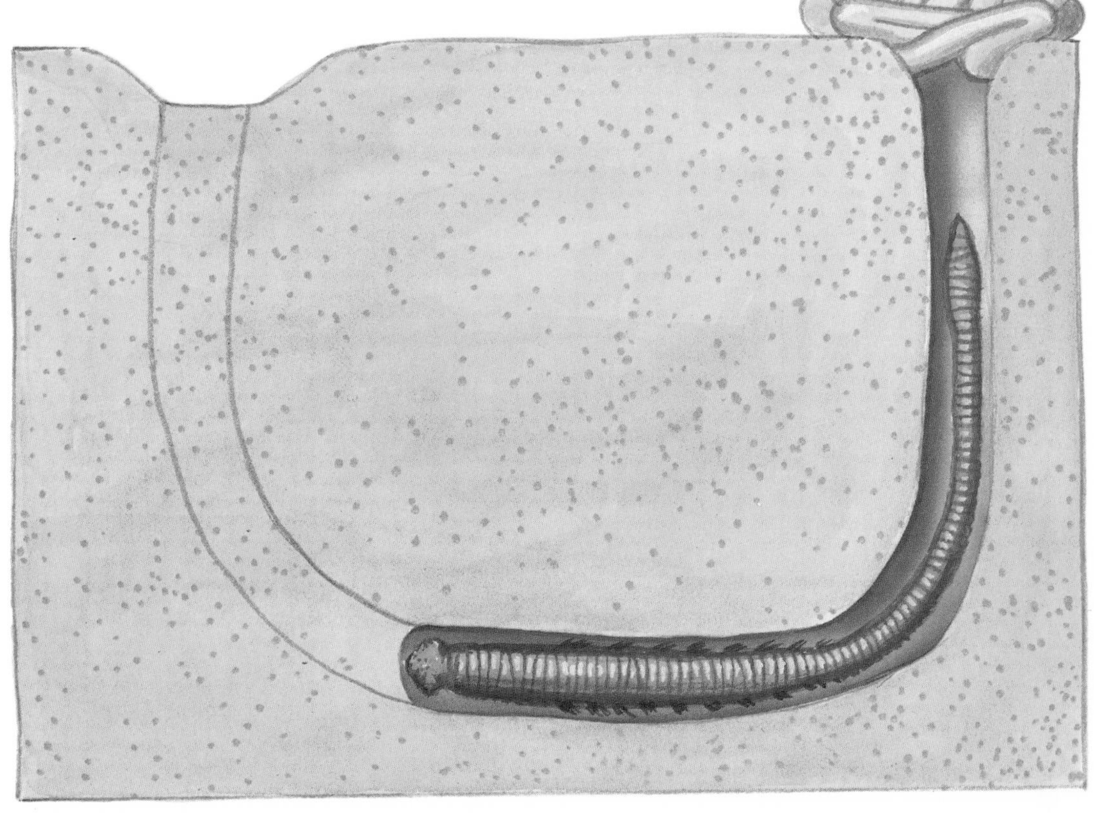

Ragworm

The ragworm is a more lively creature. This worm uses its paddle-shaped limbs to tunnel through the sand in search of food. The ragworm is *carnivorous* (kahr NIHV uhr uhs)—it eats other animals. It has a tube sticking out from its head. At the end of the tube are jaws, which grab a meal. Ragworms grow up to 3 feet (90 centimeters) long.

The beautiful peacock worm lives in a tube that sticks up from the sand. When the tide washes over the tube, the worm unfurls a ring of tentacles that catch tiny food particles floating in the water. Approximately 4 inches (10 centimeters) of the worm's body stick up

Peacock worms use their feathery tentacles to sift bits of food from the water.

The egg-shaped sea mouse is an active sea worm that hunts food on the ocean floor.

out of the sand, but another 16 inches (40 centimeters) are hidden below.

Believe it or not, the sea mouse is actually a worm that crawls through the sand. Its oval-shaped body is covered with sandy bristles and measures about 6 inches (15 centimeters) long. When the sand is washed off, the bristles change color—from gold to red to lilac to yellow to orange—depending on how the light strikes them. The sea mouse isn't too popular with other worms—if they're slower, the sea mouse eats them!

Barnacle Bit

Not all beaches are the same. Some have soft white sand. Some are created from black volcanic rock. And others are made up of flat rocks that measure about 12 inches (30.5 centimeters) across.

TREES IN THE OCEAN?

Did you know there are forests in the ocean? They're mangrove forests, and they're my kind of place—muddy, smelly, and full of friends!

Most mangroves grow along coasts in tropical regions of the world, and they're probably the weirdest shrubs you'll ever see. They look like giant spidery trees. New sprouts grow down from their branches; their roots grow down from their trunk; and other growths sprout up from the roots for oxygen.

Mangroves stand in salt water when the tide is in, and they're just as happy to stand in mud when the tide is out. Most plants can't grow in either mud or salt water, because mud doesn't give them enough oxygen, and too much salt harms them. But mangroves are different. They breathe through pores in their roots above the ground, and their roots can block salt from entering. If some salt does seep in, they excrete it through glands on their leaves.

A mangrove feeds hundreds of creatures each year, just by dropping its leaves. The leaves break down into a rich, yummy ooze for worms, shrimp, and beetles—not to mention crabs like me. You'll want to meet my cousin fiddler crab. He shovels the mud into his mouth and scrapes every grain of mud clean of edible goodies. Then fiddler rolls the clean mud into a ball and spits it out! You may not want to invite him to lunch, but he's fun to watch.

We crabs have to be careful of our mangrove neighbors, though. Some of the locals would like to eat *us*. Birds such as herons, egrets, and storks are best avoided, and so are mammals such as raccoons and muskrats. They, in turn,

Feeding in a mangrove swamp, fiddler crabs cover a muddy shore at low tide.

A mudskipper uses its fins to climb out of water onto a tree.

have to watch out for our neighborhood alligators, who see them as a tasty mouthful.

Oysters, barnacles, and mussels cling to the roots of the mangroves. People in Puerto Rico and elsewhere harvest them to eat or to sell.

Some very odd fish live in mangrove forests. The archerfish lives in Asian mangroves, between India and Australia. When the archerfish spots an insect on a mangrove leaf, it squirts the leaf with water until the insect falls from the leaf—right into the fish's mouth.

Another unusual fish, the mudskipper, lives along the Indian and Pacific oceans. The mudskipper can live outside water, provided it returns to the sea frequently to moisten its skin and fill its gills. It walks on its handlike fins on the mud at low tide. One kind of mudskipper actually climbs trees!

For many years, people thought mangroves were worse than useless—their leaves smell like rotten eggs, and their forests swarm with mosquitoes. However, today we know that mangroves are beneficial to people as well as to marine life. For example, mangrove forests provide food and shelter for many animals, especially small fish that will go farther out to sea when they are larger. In addition, mangroves provide a barrier between the land and storms at sea. In fact, every day, the mangroves help build solid land by capturing mud in their roots and slowing the movement of the tides against the land.

Barnacle Bit

When Wilson Vailoces, a farmer in the Philippines, noticed the damage being done to coastal areas, he formed a group called Sea Watchers. Volunteers patrol the coastline to stop illegal fishing methods and prevent people from destroying the coastline. Working to bring the land back in harmony with the sea, Vailoces himself has planted nearly 10,000 mangroves.

Make a Seabed Viewer

Make your own seabed viewer and explore the underwater shore, even at a pond or creek.

Things you need:

- ***a large milk or juice carton***
- ***a pair of scissors***
- ***a pencil***
- ***plastic wrap***
- ***a large rubber band***

1. Cut off the top flaps of the carton. (You may want to ask an adult to help you cut.)

2. Draw a square on the bottom of the carton, leaving a small border on all sides. Cut along the pencil lines and remove the square.

3. Place plastic wrap over the bottom of the carton and part of the sides. Pull it tight. Then slip a rubber band over the carton and plastic wrap to keep the plastic wrap in place.

4. Dip the plastic-wrapped end of the carton into calm, shallow water near the shore. If it's a sunny day, put a towel over your head to cut the glare. You may want to write in a notebook all your observations about the different kinds of living things you see.

Important: Never go into the water without a partner or a lifeguard on duty!

THE SHORE UNDERWATER

Now let's explore life in the shallow waters along the seaside. You might want to wear a pair of goggles, but I'll go just as I am. We'll start in the shallow waters off Europe, where you may not believe your eyes! Is that fish *walking* along the ocean floor? Yep, that's the tub gurnard strolling along underwater across sand, mud, and rocks.

The tub gurnard walks with the help of special rays that stick out from fins under its body. It also uses these rays as feelers to search for small fish, shrimp, crabs, and sea

A tub gurnard uses its spiny rays to walk and to feel for food on the ocean bottom.

Scallops skillfully maneuver through the water by rapidly opening and closing their shells.

worms in the sand. And this odd fish has a pointed snout that helps it suck up food from the ocean floor, too.

Let's head toward the northwestern part of Europe now, and look for a queen scallop. Be sure to keep your eyes peeled, because the queen scallop has a blotchy brown shell that blends in with the seabed.

Like other scallops, the queen scallop has a nifty two-piece shell. The two pieces are connected by some tissue, which acts as a sort of hinge. When the queen scallop wants to eat, it opens its shell and traps tiny living algae in long hairs. To protect itself, the scallop snaps its shell shut.

The lesser weever can defend itself with the spines on its long back fin. It uses them to inject its enemies with poison.

A scallop also uses its shell to swim, something it does much better than other shellfish. It opens and closes its shell rapidly, pushing itself through the water. In this way, it can escape its enemies.

Close to shore in Europe and Africa lies the lesser weever fish. I prefer to steer clear of this fish, but that's not easy. The lesser weever digs itself into the ocean floor with its fins. Then it just lies there with only its eyes, mouth, and back fin sticking out, waiting for an unsuspecting creature like myself to wander by.

Why do I want to avoid the weever? Its back fin has sharp spines that contain sacs of poison. It uses those spines like needles to inject its enemies with poison.

Barnacle Bit

The stargazer is a shocking fish of the shallows. Some species lurk in the seabed, attracting their prey with a wormlike lure on their tongue. These stargazers use special organs around their eyes to zap their enemies with a 50-volt electric shock.

The large front claw is the "gun" this pistol shrimp uses to knock out its prey with shock waves.

Another feisty creature of the shallows is the pistol shrimp, which lives in the Caribbean. The pistol shrimp gets its name from the way it snaps its one large claw to shoot shock waves at its prey. These shock waves are strong enough to stun nearby fish.

SCHOOL FOR OTTERS

To most people, California sea otters seem like carefree animals that just play in the sea all day long. But what looks like play to us is actually hard work—it's a matter of staying alive.

Normally, a mother sea otter teaches her pup the skills it needs to live. She shows the pup how to keep warm through constant grooming, and how to dine off the ocean's bounty.

Without these lessons, a baby otter would soon die. But some orphan otters are learning these vital skills from people at California's Monterey Bay Aquarium.

The aquarium's staff and volunteers take care of baby otters who have lost their mothers, either to a winter storm, pollution, or a predator. At the aquarium, the first job is to keep the baby sea otter alive by grooming its fur. Unlike other marine animals that have a thick layer of blubber, otters have little body fat to keep them warm. Otters stay warm by constantly cleaning their thick pelts. This fills the pelt with hundreds of tiny air bubbles that insulate the animal against cold. But when a baby otter's fur is matted after a long fight with the ocean, it can easily die from a big chill.

Another priority is to feed the baby otters fatty foods. Their bodies need plenty of energy to clean their pelts, and they need calories to burn to keep warm. In fact, otters need to eat about 25 percent of their body weight every day. For a 55-pound (25-kilogram) person, that would be about 14 pounds (6.5 kilograms) of food *daily*!

At the aquarium, the pups get a high-fat milkshake of squid, clams, cream, milk, salt water, cod-liver oil, vitamins, and minerals.

But before returning to the sea, the otters must go to "otter school" to learn how to forage for food on the seabed. In the wild, the mother otter teaches the pup how to dive into the water and search the rocks for crabs, mussels, or abalone. She teaches them how to dig for clams, too. Then she shows the pups how to smash the clam shells against a rock and eat the tasty flesh. At the aquarium's otter school, the orphans learn all these skills from people.

After their training, the baby otters are released into the sea. In spite of their new skills, otters in the wild face many dangers, including oil spills and overhunting. But with friends like those at the aquarium, the California sea otters' chances for survival are much improved.

A "substitute mother" gives a baby sea otter a lesson in ocean living—how to hold and eat a meal.

BIRDS OF THE SEASHORE

Least tern

Want to meet some real high fliers? You guessed it, I'm talking about birds. We're going to meet shorebirds all over the world, but I'll keep a low profile. Shorebirds see me as a spicy snack! Don't worry, I know how to protect myself. I'll use this seashell as my shield.

Ring-billed gull

Herring gull

American oystercatcher

Ruddy turnstone

Sea birds usually nest in trees, bushes, or grass on land, and rely on the ocean for food. Some birds, such as the brown pelican, dive into the water for a meal. Pelicans can be found along seacoasts worldwide. They have a long, straight bill with a large pouch of skin underneath. When a brown pelican sees fish, it dives—from as high as 70 feet (21 meters) above the sea. Air sacs under its skin cushion the bird as it hits the sea.

Semi-palmated plover

Brown pelican

The pelican scoops up fish-filled water, drains the water from its pouch, and lifts its bill so that the fish slip into its belly.

Another bird that swoops over water is the gull. Sea gulls live on coasts throughout the world. These birds use their strong, hooked beaks to eat anything—bugs, dead animals, garbage, and fish, as well as the eggs and chicks of other birds. A gull can steal the fish right out of another bird's bill!

The black-headed gull wades along the shore seeking its meal. It uses its webbed feet to paddle rapidly in one spot. Then it hops back and catches anything that scurries out of the water. And then there are herring gulls. Herring gulls make me nervous. These gulls like to grab a crab, soar into the sky, and then drop the crab on rocks to smash open its shell.

Barnacle Bit

How does our water pollution affect birds? It's a chain reaction: When people use harsh chemicals on land, rain washes the chemicals into the sea, where they get into the bodies of fish. When birds eat the fish, the chemicals get into their bodies. Some contaminated birds die. Others live, but they produce eggs with thin shells. The eggs easily break, and few baby birds are hatched.

Wading birds graze for food, usually along sandy or muddy shores. A wading bird's choice of food depends on the size and shape of its bill. I stay clear of the crab plover, which lives along the shores of the Indian Ocean. This bird uses its bill as a hammer to smash the shells of—that's right—crabs!

Sanderlings look for food left on the beach at low tide.

You can see sandpipers all around the world. They use their long bills to dig deep in the sand and nab ragworms and lugworms. Sanderlings—their close relations—have shorter bills. When the tide goes out, sanderlings race up and down the beach, chasing the waves and plucking shellfish and insects left behind by the ebbing waters.

Although most wading birds prefer to eat on sandy shores, the oystercatcher likes rocky shores. Oystercatchers use their sharp, chisel-shaped bills to open the shells of mussels, clams, crabs, and, of course, oysters. When this bird sees an oyster with its shell open, it darts its bill into the oyster's shell and cuts the muscle that closes the shell. Then it eats the animal. If the oyster closes its shell around the oystercatcher's beak, the bird hits it against a rock until the shell cracks.

All this talk about cracking shells is making me queasy. I think it's time to go!

Barnacle Bit

The roseate spoonbill, a wading bird that lives in warm parts of North and South America, is a sight to see. It has a pink body; an orange tail; red eyes; and a broad, flat bill, which it swings from side to side in the water to gather food.

SEA LAB

Sink or Fly?

Sea birds have special oils and feathers that allow them to fly and to swim. But sometimes people pollute waters with detergents. To see how the chemicals can harm sea birds, try this experiment.

Things you need:

- ***1 glass bowl***
- ***1 cup (250 ml) water***
- ***1 teaspoon (5 ml) cooking oil***
- ***2 teaspoons (10 ml) powdered laundry detergent***

1. Pour the water into the bowl. Watch closely as you add the oil.

2. What do you see? The oil and water don't mix. The oil lies on top of the water, because it's lighter than water. Sea birds rely on this fact to keep dry as they fish for food. Oils from special glands in the birds' skin make their feathers waterproof.

3. Now sprinkle the detergent into the oily water. Stir slowly. What do you see? Right! The detergent lets oil and water mix.

If a bird dives into water that contains a lot of detergent, the bird's natural waterproofing is destroyed. Then water seeps into the bird's feathers. If its feathers get too water-soaked and heavy, the bird sinks into the water and drowns.

SHALLOW OCEAN

Welcome to my home, the shallow ocean. I'm Inkfred Octavius Octopus—just call me Inky. I have very sharp eyes and can change my colors and squirt ink if we get into trouble, so I'm your perfect guide. Grab my arm—any arm will do—and off we go.

WHAT IS THE OCEAN'S GIANT SHELF?

What makes the shallow ocean shallow? There is a giant shelf under the water.

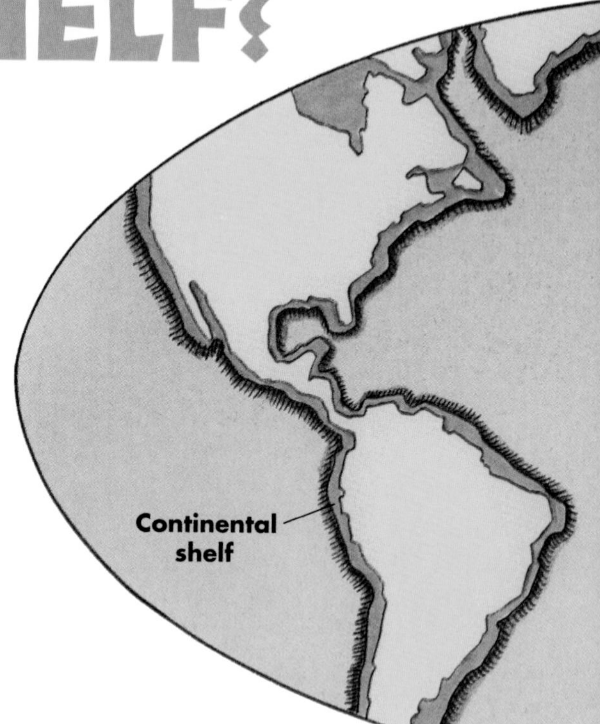

The continents don't end at the shore. Their edges continue out under the ocean, where they form the *continental shelf*. The shelf extends as far as 750 miles (1,200 kilometers) in the Arctic Ocean and as little as 1 mile (1.6 kilometers) in the Pacific. The ocean also gets shallow around islands.

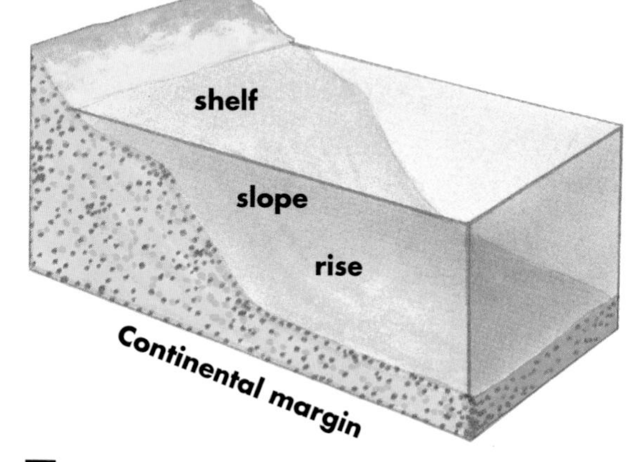

The continental shelf is part of an even larger area called the *continental margin*. It includes the continental shelf, the continental slope, and the continental rise.

The giant shelf slopes gently down from the shore. On average, the water at the lower edge is about 430 feet (130 meters) deep—that's pretty shallow for the ocean. Where the shelf ends, the water gets very deep, very fast.

And there is sunlight here too. In some places, such as the clear waters of the tropics, light reaches all the way to the bottom. Many seaweeds and other algae grow in this sunlight.

Rachel Carson, shown below with her nephew in 1960, was a famous scientist who loved the sea. She wrote, "The continental shelf is [part] of the sea, yet of all regions of the ocean it is most like the land." It has hills and valleys, rocks and gravel, and sand, of course.

In fact, most of the living things in the sea—from the tiniest to the largest—are found in the shallow ocean. Even using eight arms I can't count them all!

FOOD FOR ALL

Many people eat fish for dinner. But what do fish and other ocean creatures eat?

Plankton is the main food source in the ocean. All kinds of marine animals, from clams to whales, eat plankton. Even other plankton eat plankton! Then these creatures are eaten by larger animals, which are eaten by even bigger animals. This system is a *food web*, and plankton is at the base of it.

The many kinds of microscopic living things in plankton make it a nourishing "soup" for larger ocean creatures.

Plankton is a "soup" of tiny living things. It contains bacteria, algae, tiny animals, and eggs and larvae of larger animals such as crabs, barnacles, lobsters, and sea urchins. A gallon of seawater may contain thousands or even millions of these important *organisms* (living things).

The word *plankton* comes from a Greek word that means "wandering." Some plankton can

WATER WORD

In the ocean, if you're not plankton you're probably nekton. *Nekton* consists of all the animals of the ocean that swim strongly enough to move independent of ocean currents.

swim, but they aren't strong enough to swim against the ocean currents. So plankton "wander," or drift, wherever the currents take them.

Scientists divide plankton into two main groups—phytoplankton (FY toh PLANGK tuhn) and zooplankton (ZOH uh PLANGK tuhn). *Zooplankton* consists of animals. But *phytoplankton* is more important because, like plants on land, these organisms make their own food from sunlight and nutrients. And just as animals on land can't live without plants, creatures in the ocean can't live without phytoplankton.

I like to eat crabs and lobster. But when a fish tries to eat *me*, I release my ink. Quick, hide in the cloud! Don't worry, it'll wash off.

BEAUTIFUL BUILDING BLOCKS

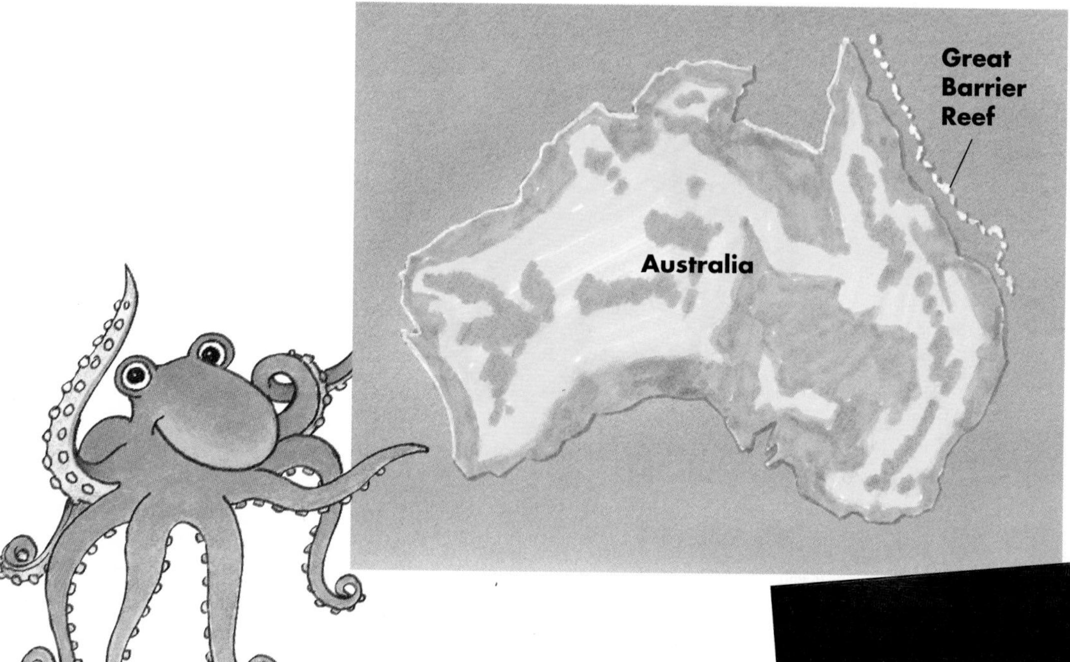

Here we are, in the shallow ocean off Australia. It's the home of the Great Barrier Reef, the world's largest group of coral reefs. The Great Barrier Reef is about 1,250 miles (2,010 kilometers) long, the largest structure ever made by living creatures. Let me explain.

Have you ever seen a piece of coral? It grows throughout the sunlit coastal ocean. Coral is a hard limestone formation, kind of like a rock. Different kinds of coral come in different colors.

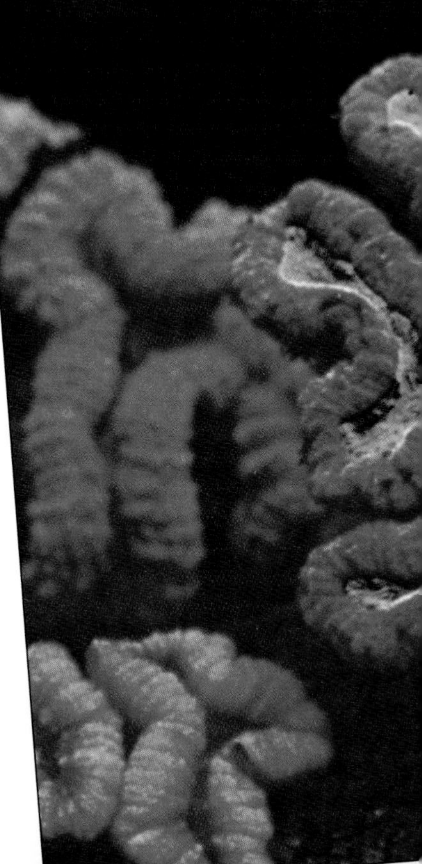

Just look—fiery red, bright white, mellow yellow, cool blue, keen green, royal purple—a whole rainbow! There is even a bright fluorescent coral. Some kinds of coral are so beautiful that people display it in their homes or wear coral jewelry.

Coral has many different shapes, too. Some corals are shaped like fans, or domes, or tiny organ pipes, or even antlers. Those that look like plants have names to match—for example, "mushroom coral" and "lettuce coral." One kind

Coral islands like this one are part of the Great Barrier Reef in Australia.

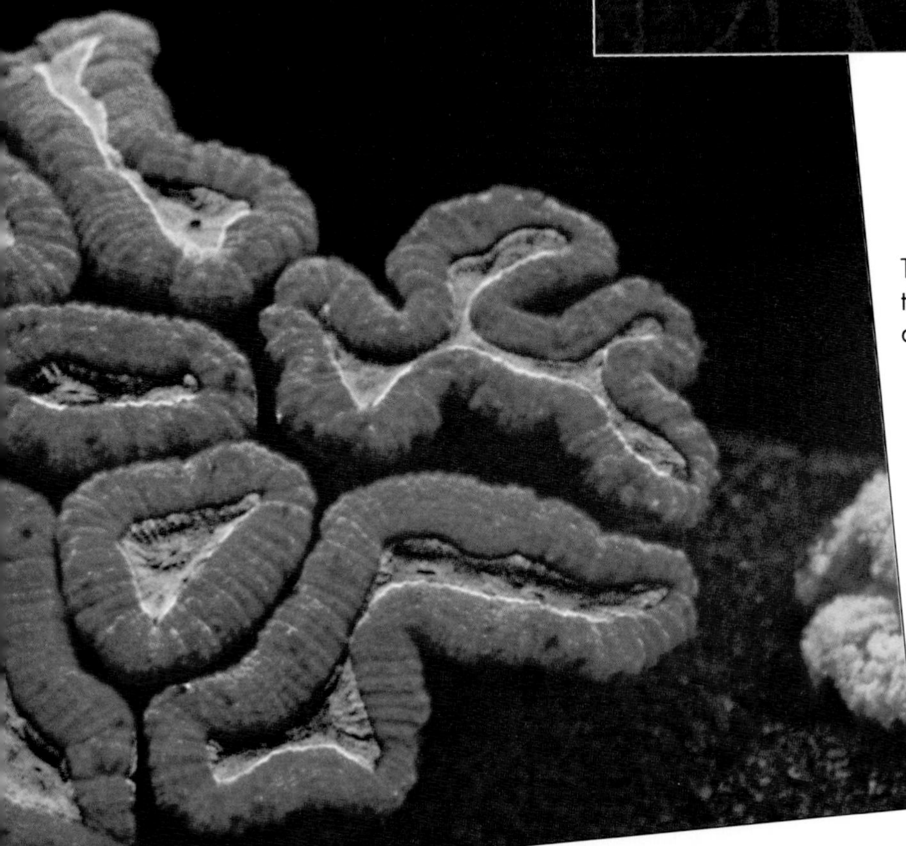

The living animals in this fluorescing coral actually glow.

Coral polyp

is called "brain coral" because it looks like a human brain.

Unlike other rocky substances, coral is formed by tiny animals—*coral polyps*. Most polyps are very small, less than 1 inch (2.5 centimeters) in diameter, and they're shaped like tubes. They use one end of their body to eat plankton and waste products from other living things. They use the other end to anchor themselves to the skeletons of dead polyps.

Coral polyps form their skeletons from minerals in the water. When a polyp dies, its skeleton remains. New polyps grow from eggs or little buds sent out by adult polyps, and they attach themselves to these skeletons. They build their own skeletons right on top of the old ones.

The leaf shape of cabbage coral is only one of the unusual forms developed by different coral species.

Transparent polyps extend from a colony of bubble coral in the Red Sea.

Some coral polyps live alone or in small groups, but often they live in enormous groups—millions and trillions of them! Their skeletons build up into underwater structures called reefs, or ridges. A typical reef might grow about 20 inches (50 centimeters) higher every fifty years. Over thousands and even millions of years, coral reefs can get pretty big. How many *trillions* of tiny polyps did it take to form the Great Barrier Reef? No one will ever know exactly, but scientists say it took as long as 6 million years to make it.

There are about 60,000 miles (97,000 kilometers) of reefs in the warm, tropical waters of the Pacific and Indian oceans, and in parts of the Atlantic, including the Caribbean Sea.

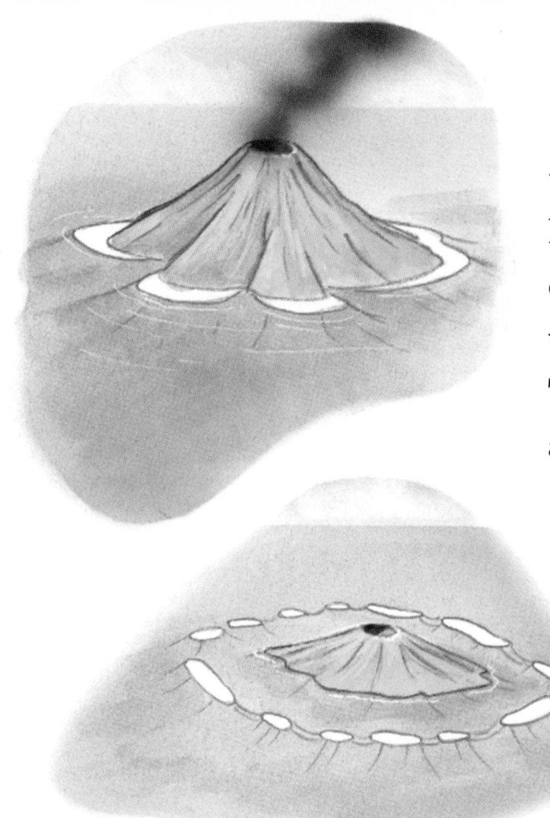

Depending on how and where they form, coral reefs have different names. Some are called *fringing reefs* because they grow at the fringes of land. They extend from the shore out a short distance into the sea.

Atolls (AT ohlz) are reefs that turn into islands. They start as fringing reefs that form around a volcano in the ocean.

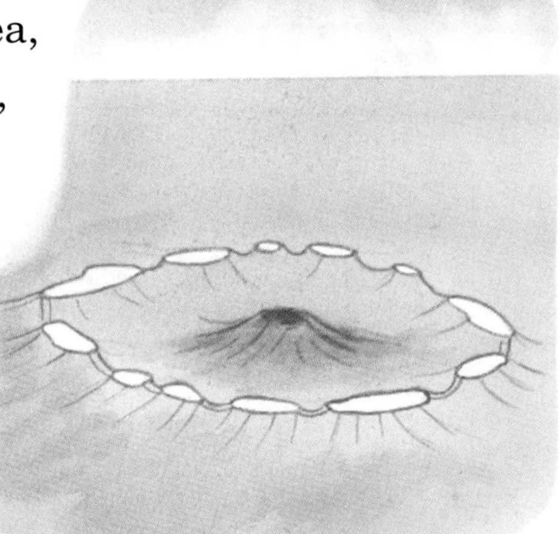

When the volcano sinks into the sea, the circular reef remains above water, forming a ring-shaped island or atoll.

Most atolls are found in the Pacific Ocean, in areas where volcanoes most frequently form. The shallow water enclosed by the atoll is called a *lagoon*.

Barrier reefs, like the Great Barrier Reef of Australia, form a wall between the open ocean and the water near the shoreline.

Every coral reef is home to many kinds of sea life—including octopuses. Let's meet some of my neighbors.

THE CORAL REEF COMMUNITY

Coral reefs cover only about 1/500 of the ocean floor, but they are home to 1/4 of all the plants and animals of the sea. Yes, I live in a busy, colorful neighborhood.

Did you see that bright red grouper flash by? And look at all those golden fairy basselets.

There are always schools of fish darting around coral reefs. We have fish called grunts here that actually make a grunting noise. And

Corals, a large grouper, and much smaller fairy basselets are part of a coral reef community in the Red Sea.

there are rainbow-colored angelfish, and blue-striped damselfish, and—uh-oh—here's a sand shark cruising by! Let's find a good place to hide!

One big reason so many creatures live in coral reefs is that there are plenty of cracks and crevices and tunnels to use for homes and hiding places. Now, aren't you glad you're here?

That parrotfish may look like an underwater bird. But instead of squawking, it crunches on the coral to find food. The shark's gone, so let's swim out and see who else is around.

Sea anemones are a common sight on coral reefs. These animals look like the flowers called anemones, but their cylinder-shaped bodies are topped with poisonous tentacles. Sea anemones sting fish with their tentacles and then pull the unlucky fish into their mouths.

Most sea creatures avoid the sea anemone—but clownfish live among those deadly tentacles. It's the perfect hiding place, because very few animals dare to swim there. Somehow, clownfish can safely rub against the anemones and protect themselves. The mucus that covers the anemone rubs off on the clownfish and on the eggs it lays. To the anemone, the mucous coating feels just like itself so it doesn't sting the clownfish.

Clownfish need anemones to survive, but anemones need clownfish, too. The clownfish chases other animals away from its territory, including animals that might eat the anemone. Sometimes clownfish

A crown-of-thorns starfish feeds on living coral. If its numbers increase, large areas of the reef may die.

even feed anemones by bringing them dead fish. The clownfish and the anemone are partners.

Such partnerships exist throughout a coral reef community. When creatures help each other like this, the partnership is called *symbiosis* (SIHM by OH sihs), which means "living together."

Barnacle Bit

Symbiosis exists between fish called gobies and some kinds of shrimp. The shrimp digs a burrow on the sea floor and shares its home with a goby. In return, the goby acts as a lookout. With a flick of its tail, the goby warns the shrimp of an approaching enemy.

But even here, the food web is in action. Watch out for the moray eel. It's 6 feet (1.8 meters) long and looks like a snake. It hides in crevices, waiting to strike out at unsuspecting fish.

Those pretty crown-of-thorns starfish are killers, too. They eat live coral. Sometimes the population of crown-of-thorns starfish suddenly rises. When that happens, the starfish can kill most of the reef and destroy the homes of thousands of reef creatures.

It's getting dark now. Watch what happens. At night, different animals patrol the reef. Strange, glow-in-the-dark fish swim out of their daytime hiding places. Snails and crabs crawl across the ocean floor. The whole reef changes when the "night shift" takes over.

Many people say coral reefs look like beautiful undersea gardens. They're right. I wouldn't live anywhere else. But coral reefs are in trouble. Come with me and see why.

Moray eel

A night-feeding spider crab feeds on soft polyps of living coral.

SAVING THE REEFS

Many people enjoy diving to see the stunning beauty of the reefs. Scientists come to study us and to collect seaweeds and animals. They've learned that certain chemicals in marine organisms help fight diseases in people.

People like reefs for other reasons, too. Barrier reefs protect beaches from waves that would otherwise wash the sand away. And the fish around reefs provide a lot of food. Many countries get one-fourth of their fish—tuna, mackerel, snapper, and others—near reefs.

Sometimes natural forces, such as hurricanes, devastate a coral reef. Over time, the area rebuilds itself as part of nature's cycle. But some humans damage our wonderful home and don't let it recover.

More than half of all the world's people live in coastal areas. To develop the land, they cut down trees, especially mangrove forests. Without trees to hold it in place, the soil and other sediment is washed by rain into the shallow ocean, where it settles on reefs. This often smothers the coral and prevents new coral from growing. Without the coral, the food web is disrupted and much of the reef community may die.

Pollutants dumped into the water and chemicals washed from the land also hurt coral reefs. And huge sections of reefs are destroyed when they are mined for limestone or exploded by fishing crews, who scoop up the stunned fish.

Today, truly healthy reefs are those that are protected from human activity.

Strategically anchored docks *(below)* and carefully guided tours *(right)* help protect the reef community while tourists experience its natural beauty.

CUCUMBERS IN A PICKLE

The Galapagos (guh LAH puh GOHS) Islands make up a beautiful chain of volcanic islands in the Pacific Ocean off the coast of Ecuador. The Galapagos are famous for their unusual wildlife, especially marine iguanas—the only lizards that feed in the ocean—and giant tortoises, land turtles that may weigh up to 600 pounds (270 kilograms).

Look in the shallow waters off the islands and you may find sea cucumbers covering the ocean floor. We're not talking about vegetables. Sea cucumbers are animals that feed on the sediment which drifts from the land to the ocean floor. The species here is brownish and about 10 inches (25 centimeters) long. At one end is its mouth, with tentacles that help it catch its microscopic food. Along its body are five double rows of tiny "tube feet" with little suction disks. The tube feet help the sea cucumber crawl along the rocks and sand of the sea floor to look for food.

But someone is looking for them! Remember the food web? Many people find sea cucumbers delicious. In China and other Asian countries, sea cucumbers are boiled and then dried to make *trepang* (trih PANG), which is used in soups and other dishes.

In the Galapagos, fishermen called *pepiñeros* (PAY pee NYAY rohs) make money by catching and selling sea cucumbers. The pepiñeros harvest as many as 150,000 of them each day.

This may be good for the pepiñeros, but it's hard on the sea cucumber population. Scientists say the sea cucumbers will die out in a few years if the pepiñeros aren't stopped. There won't be enough sea cucumbers to produce young and replace themselves.

To make matters worse, the pepiñeros go ashore on small islands to prepare the sea cucumbers for shipment. The balance of nature on these islands is easily upset. For example, when the pepiñeros land their boats, rats sometimes jump ship and invade the islands. The rats eat birds' eggs and compete with other animals for food. Pepiñeros also cut down trees to make fires to dry the sea cucumbers, but they don't plant new ones.

The pepiñeros say they're just trying to make a living—sea cucumbers are about twenty times more valuable than other creatures they could catch. But to protect the sea cucumbers and the islands, the Galapagos's government stepped in. Sea cucumber fishing was banned.

The situation in the Galapagos shows how human needs and the need to conserve natural treasures can come into conflict.

A pepiñero equipped with diving gear harvests sea cucumbers.

UNDERWATER FOREST

Have you ever been in an underwater forest? One made of seaweed?

Giant kelp grows more than 150 feet (46 meters) high. That's taller than a fifteen-story building. Where many giant kelps grow together, they form a kelp forest. The kelps grow from a hard sea floor in cool ocean water from 20 to 80 feet (6 to 24 meters) deep. Their beautiful *blades* (leaflike parts) sway with the ocean currents, like trees in the wind. Near the surface, the blades intertwine, creating a canopy that moves up and down with the waves. The sunlight and shadow play among the golden-brown seaweed.

Kelp forests, like coral reefs, shelter thousands of living things. One giant kelp forest off California's coast is home to about 800 species of plants and animals! Fish, snails, scallops, and other sea creatures feed on the kelp and hide in it. Many spend their whole lives here. Other types of

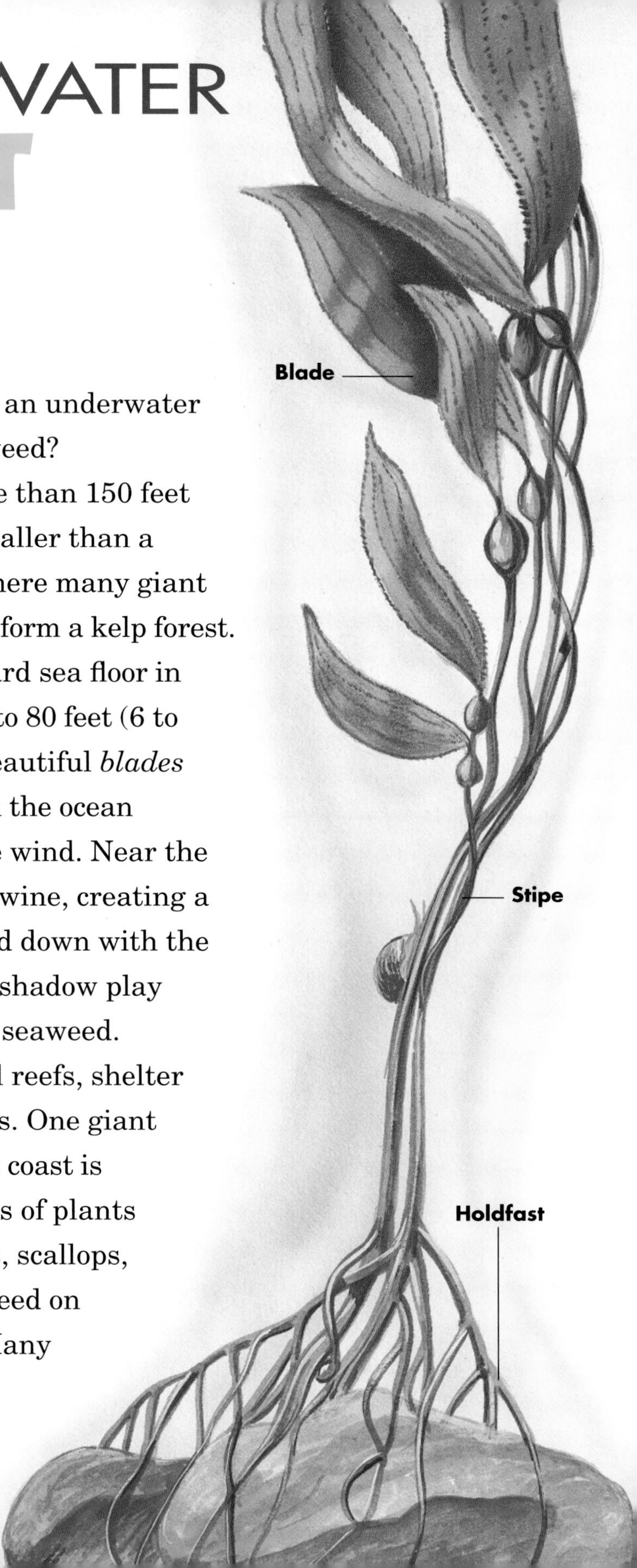

Blade
Stipe
Holdfast

A diver explores a kelp forest off the coast of California.

seaweeds grow here, too. Who else lives here? Dive down to the bottom and work your way up.

On the hard ocean floor, each kelp is anchored by a holdfast. The *holdfast* anchors the kelp to keep it from being carried away by the ocean currents. A holdfast looks like a tangle of roots, but its main job is to hold the kelp to the ocean floor. Unlike the roots of plants, it isn't the only part to take up minerals and water. Instead, the whole seaweed takes in nutrients. The animals that live in holdfasts don't

Brittle star

care, though. They just know they've found a good home.

A holdfast may be home to dozens of brittle stars. These creatures look like little sea stars. Some people call them serpent stars because, at times, their long arms look like snakes. Brittle stars use their arms to walk along the ocean floor, searching for food. Big orange sea stars that hang on the outside of the holdfast are called bat stars. Sometimes you'll see mussels, hermit crabs, and worms there, too.

Bat stars cling to and feed on the holdfast of this kelp plant.

Kelp crabs like this one cling to the stemlike stipes of kelp.

Swim up a little higher along the giant kelp. The stemlike parts of the kelp, called *stipes* (styps), grow up from the holdfasts. All along the length of the kelp, you'll see living creatures such as crabs and snails. For instance, topsnails crawl on the stipes and graze on the algae there.

All kinds of beautiful fish—kelp bass, yellow-and-green perch, and bright orange garibaldis—swim through this enchanted forest, like birds flying among trees on land. Farther up the kelp forest, in the canopy, you can see blue rockfish

This sea otter has wrapped itself in kelp blades and is ready for a nap.

munching on plankton, and kelp clingfish holding onto the kelp with their special fins.

On the ocean surface, sea otters live among the tangled mats of kelp. They like to wrap themselves in the blades and sleep there. Sea lions swim there, too.

But sea creatures aren't the only ones who benefit from a kelp forest. People do, too. Do you like ice cream? Did you know it has kelp in it? Many chemical substances come from kelp. One of them keeps ice crystals from forming in your "rocky road." I'm sure you use toothpaste, too. Kelp extracts give some toothpastes their creamy texture. And even the furniture polish you use has kelp in it. Kelp keeps it smooth and creamy.

So you could say you're practically surrounded by kelp every day.

People harvest wild kelp or grow it in special sea farms. Some kelp grows fast—almost 100 feet (30 meters) a year. How much did you grow last year? At its peak, kelp can grow 24 inches (60 centimeters) in a single day!

Even though kelp is used in hundreds of products, what I love most is the beauty of the kelp forest. Many people appreciate its beauty, too. Do you think those divers over there know that giant kelp is the largest algae in all the ocean? Let's swim over to them and ask.

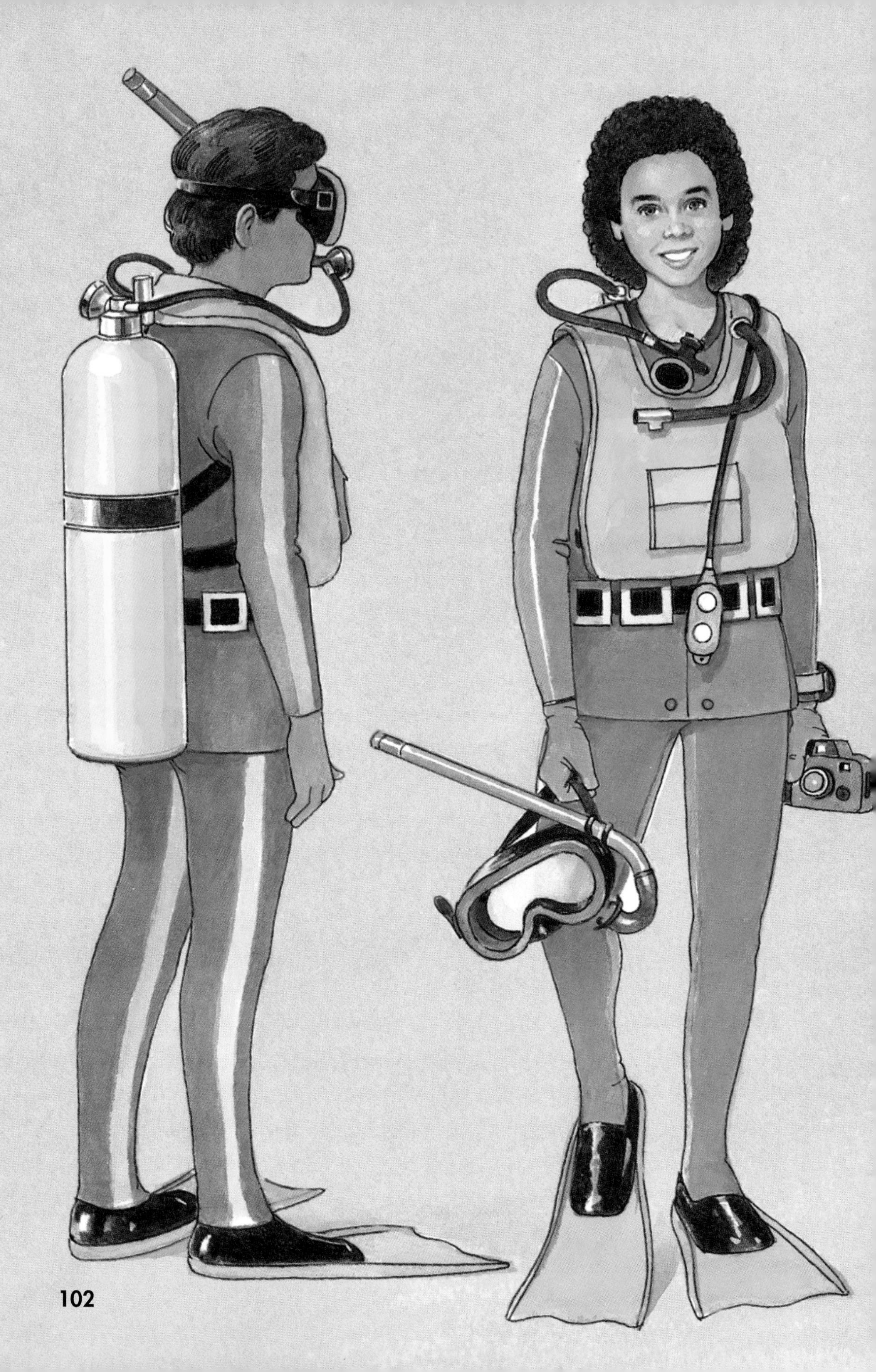

ON YOUR OWN

Today you're touring the ocean with me, but if you visit on your own, you'll need to prepare. Let's talk to Kate and Manuel.

"Hi Kate! Hi Manuel! Got any tips for us about the kind of diving you're doing?"

"Hi Inky! There sure is plenty to learn before you go diving. We went to a diving school to learn it. We're both certified divers—we passed the course and got the experience we need to dive safely.

"For instance, the water gets pretty chilly down below, so we use wet suits. In fact, a wet suit will not only help keep your body warm, but it will also protect you from the small cuts, bumps, and bites of sea life. Right, Manuel?"

"Right, Kate. You'll also have to eat foods that give you lots of energy, because diving burns up calories fast. And don't be in a hurry when you dive—not just because there is so much to see, but also because it takes time for your body to adjust to the different pressure down below. Kate, tell Inky what you're wearing."

"These flippers on my feet help me swim farther and faster. And I'm wearing a face mask to help me see.

"These tanks are filled with air. They're heavy and clumsy on land, but they weigh almost nothing underwater.

"Unlike you, Inky, we human beings can't breathe underwater. The part that connects the diver to the tank, is called a *demand regulator*. It has a hose and valves that supply the right amount of air, so the diver can stay underwater for up to an hour or more. This gives the diver time to make observations and collections."

"Do you always need all that stuff when you dive in the shallow sea, Kate?"

"No, today we're scuba diving. *Scuba* stands for *s*elf-*c*ontained *u*nderwater *b*reathing

BARNACLE BIT

Can you imagine diving deep in the ocean without lots of equipment? The *ama divers* of Japan have been doing it for centuries. Somehow they have trained their bodies. They hold their breath and dive 90 feet (27 meters) or more to harvest shellfish and seaweed, using no more than a mask or goggles, and sometimes flippers.

apparatus. But sometimes I don't use an air tank at all. When we go *snorkeling*, I wear my fins, my face mask, and a snorkel. A snorkel is a tube with a mouthpiece that I breathe through while my face is in the water. I use it at the surface when I'm scuba diving, too. I can swim along the surface and look at the wonders below. Or, I can take a deep breath through the snorkel, hold it, and dive down. I can stay underwater for as long as I can hold my breath—about 90 seconds. Then it's time to come back to the surface to blow the water out of the snorkel and breathe in more air.

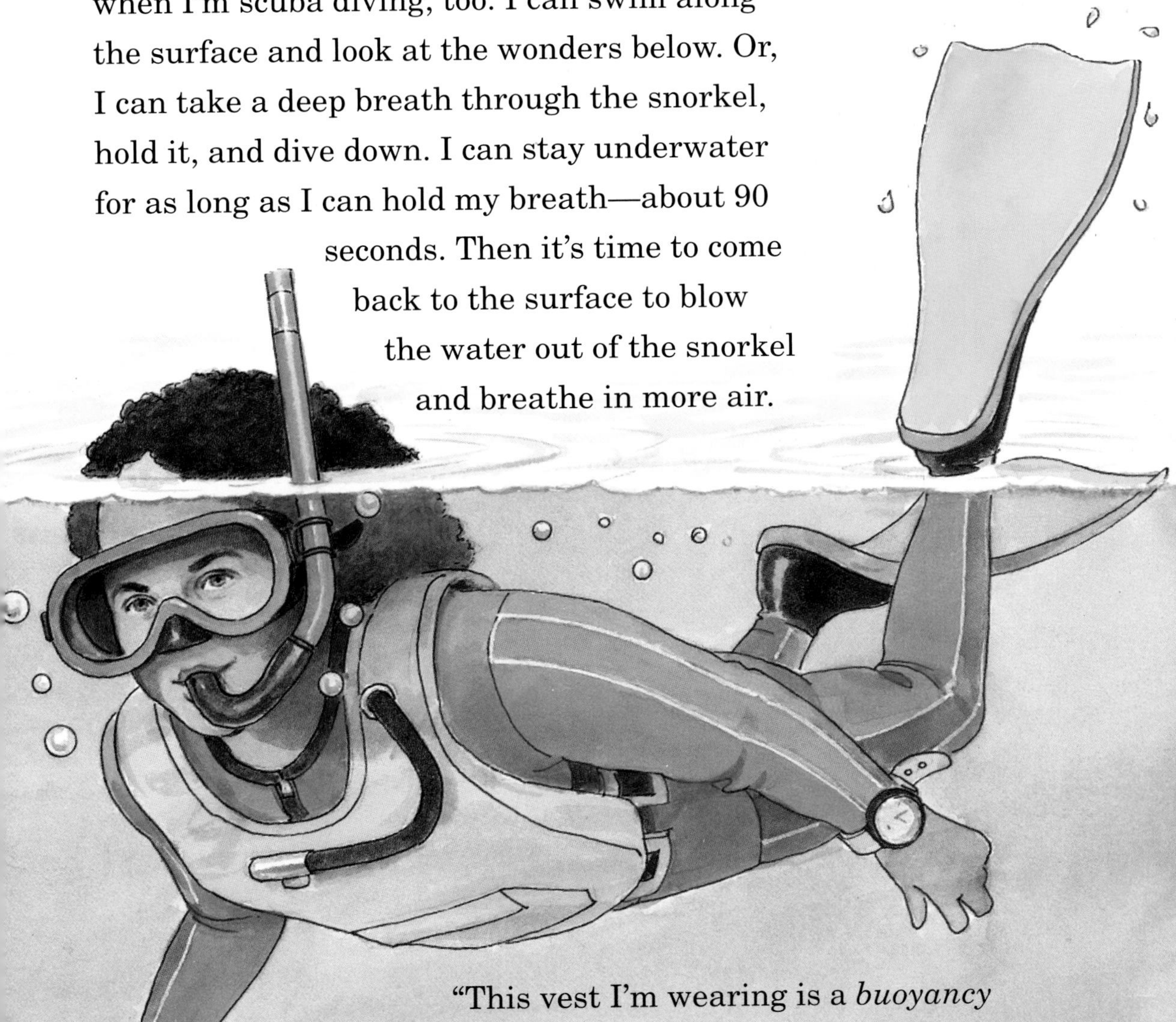

"This vest I'm wearing is a *buoyancy compensator*. It helps me stay at the depth I want instead of floating to the surface—but if I do want to float on the surface, I can inflate it. I'm wearing a weighted belt, too.

But some diving requires even more gear than we're wearing today. Tell Inky about that, Manuel."

"People who do *surface-supplied diving* wear a lot of gear. They have weighted shoes to help keep them down and helmets with hoses that go all the way to the surface. Pumps send air down to the diver through the hose. These divers can stay underwater much longer and can do heavy work, on an oil platform for example, while they are there."

"Hey, I see some damselfish. Let's take a look. Bye, Inky! Remember, when you dive, always bring a buddy!"

Wearing a weighted suit and hooked to an air pump on the ship, this surface-supplied diver is ready to be lowered to an underwater job.

Under Pressure

As water gets deeper, water pressure increases. Do this experiment, and see for yourself.

Things you need:

- ***an empty juice carton***
- ***a nail***
- ***masking tape***

1. Use the nail to poke 3 holes in one side of the carton—at the top, middle, and bottom. (Have an adult help you.)

2. Cover the holes with masking tape and place the carton in a sink.

3. Fill the carton with water. Hold it over the sink, then quickly remove the tape. What do you observe?

The lower the hole, the farther the water spurts out. Why? Because the water pressure in your juice carton increases with depth, just like the water pressure in the ocean. Water presses down on all the water underneath it. In the shallow ocean, there is less water pressing down, so there is less water pressure.

OPEN OCEAN

Glad to meet you! My name's Salty. I'm a dolphin, and I live in the open ocean. That's one great place to play. Grab my fin. I'll show you around. We'll see whales, sharks, sailfish, wahoos, tuna, squid, turtles, birds, and scads of tiny creatures just hanging out.

And that's not all! Dive in!

WHAT IS THE **OPEN OCEAN?**

What is life like in the open ocean, away from rocky shores, sandy shallows, and coral reefs? Let's find out. We'll catch an ocean current and just go with the flow.

Winds blowing over the ocean push the water into *currents*—streams that run like giant moving belts in large, roughly circular patterns. All sorts of living things ride the currents from one part of the ocean to another.

To help us understand the huge ocean, oceanographers divide it into zones. I stay mainly in the *sunlit zone* and the upper part of the *twilight zone*. The sunlit zone is the layer of water extending from the surface down to approximately 650 feet (200 meters). That's about as far down as the light from the sun reaches. The twilight zone extends from the bottom of the sunlit zone to about 3,300 feet (1,000 meters).

The deeper we go, the darker it gets. As sunlight streams down through the ocean water, more and more of the sun's rays are filtered out. Red and orange are filtered out in the upper layers.

If you scraped your skin 100 feet (30.5 meters) down, your blood would look green!

Farther down, yellow and green disappear. In the twilight zone, only blue remains.

Finally, we're in total darkness.

The sunlit zone is a busy place. This layer of the ocean has enough sunlight for algae and seaweed to grow. It's also full of swimming things of all shapes and sizes, from microscopic animals to whales. The sunlit zone is like a big cupboard—full of goodies for ocean creatures.

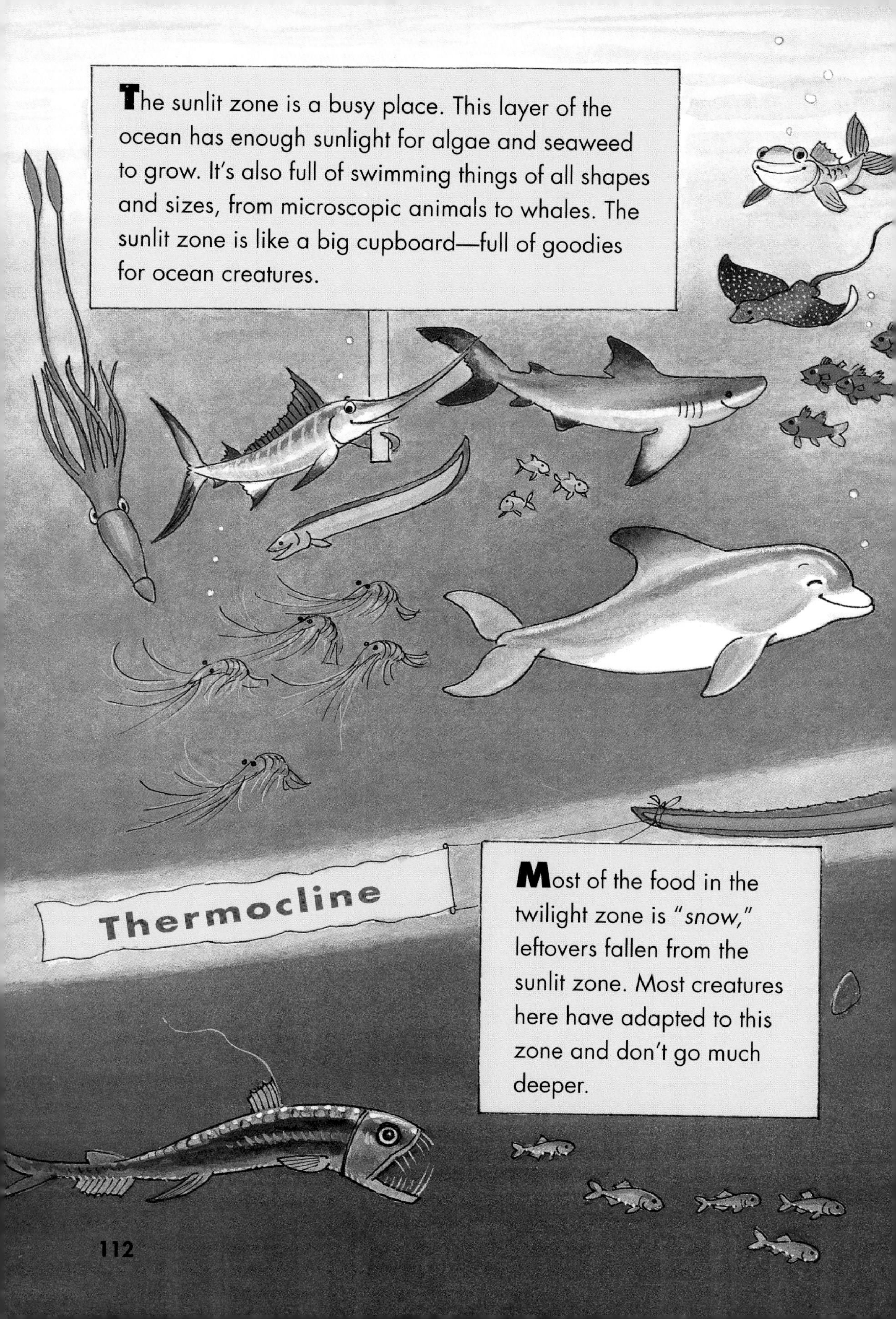

Thermocline

Most of the food in the twilight zone is "*snow,*" leftovers fallen from the sunlit zone. Most creatures here have adapted to this zone and don't go much deeper.

Are you feeling chilly? Temperatures on the ocean surface vary a lot, but as we go down, they get steadier—and colder. Generally, the open ocean has a top layer of warmer, lighter, well-mixed water and a deeper layer of cold, still, heavy water. Between them is the *thermocline,* a layer where the temperature and the *density,* or heaviness, of the water change quickly.

In the tropics, the thermocline keeps the warm layer and the cold layer separate most of the time. But in cold parts of the world, or places with changing seasons, the thermocline sometimes cools down and disappears. Then the layers mix.

AT THE SURFACE

A diver visits a school of tuna jack in the sunlit zone.

Remember plankton, the most important members of the ocean world? Like larger sea animals, certain zooplankton migrate—but they migrate up and down. After dark, these zooplankton rise up near the ocean surface, feeding on nutrients—or on other plankton. Fish, marine mammals, and birds follow and then feed on *them* during the night. When morning comes, the surviving zooplankton head below.

What kinds of fish cruise the open ocean? Look for tuna, wahoo, mackerel, sailfish, marlin, swordfish, and others. These sleek, fast-swimming fish travel thousands of miles all around the world looking for food.

Zooplankton

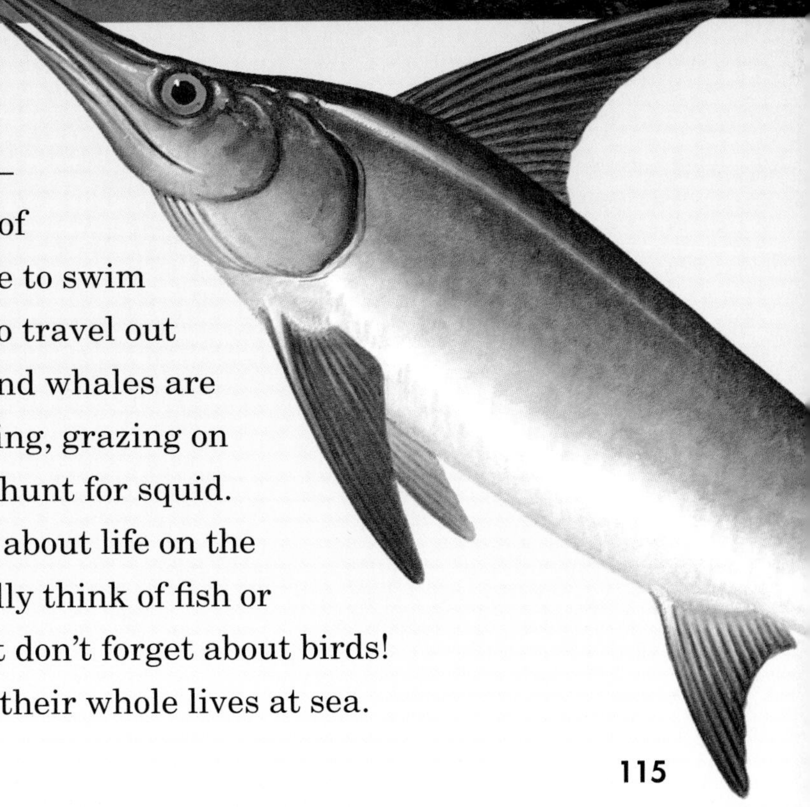

You'll see lots of dolphins out here too—I have about 40 kinds of cousins. Most of us like to swim near shore, but we also travel out into the open ocean. And whales are here of course, migrating, grazing on plankton, or diving to hunt for squid.

When people think about life on the open ocean, they usually think of fish or marine mammals. But don't forget about birds! Some sea birds spend their whole lives at sea.

Barnacle Bit

Scientists have recorded albatrosses traveling 6,000 miles (9,660 kilometers). And giant petrels have been found to roam an amazing 10,000 miles (16,000 kilometers) at sea.

They return to favorite islands or cliffs for only a few weeks each year to breed and raise their young.

Some people think of sea gulls as sea birds. But when you see a gull, you can expect to see land, because sea gulls almost always hug the shore. They live near water, but not on it.

Puffins waddle like clumsy clowns around their nesting grounds, and they glide for hours on a strong wind. But on the ocean, where they spend eight months of the year, their small wings work better as sleek flippers. They beat up and down to propel the puffin after a darting fish. Puffins are also fishing machines! The puffin's mouth and beak are shaped so that it can carry and catch fish at the same time. A puffin can hold more than 20 small fish in its mouth and still catch more.

Northern gannets take to the sea as fledglings about 13 weeks old, and they never return to land except at nesting time. Large, stout-bodied albatrosses glide on the wind for hours, then settle to float on the waves, waiting for their favorite snack, squid, to surface at night. They also follow ships to eat scraps tossed overboard.

Graceful terns zip through the air just above the water's surface, heads cocked downward, scanning for fish. They hover, dive, snatch small

Long, trailing tail feathers make this tropicbird easy to spot as it soars above warm ocean waters.

fish at the surface, then quickly wing away with their fresh catch. Little storm-petrels, the smallest sea birds, are no bigger than a swallow, but they live on the high seas. When looking for plankton and other tasty morsels, they seem to walk on the water, holding out their wings and paddling their feet along the top of the waves.

Tropicbirds, flying high over warm tropical waters, can be identified by their two extra-long, slender central tail feathers—sometimes bright red. Tropicbirds plunge from great heights to grab a squid or fish.

I haven't even mentioned the auks, fulmars, shearwaters, pelicans, and all the rest. There's a lot of life on the wing out here!

SEA LAB

Dating a Fish

How long does a fish live? Here's one way to find out.

Things you need:

- ***scales from a fish***
- ***a magnifying glass or microscope***
- ***a piece of dark paper***

1. Ask for a few fish scales at the supermarket.

2. Place a scale on the dark paper. Look at it through the magnifying glass. You should see rings with wide bands.

3. Count the wide bands, each of which represents one year. That's how old the fish scale is—and probably the fish, too.

This fish-dating method works best on fish that live in places with warm and cold seasons. For these fish, most growth takes place in warm weather, making a wide band on the scale. In colder weather, growth slows way down, making only a thin darker "edge."

Scale-dating gives you an exact age for the scale, but only a good guess at the age of the fish. If they're bitten or bumped, fish sometimes lose scales and develop new ones to fill in the spot.

RECORD BREAKERS

Ladies and gentlemen, start your fins and flippers! Time to show what you can do! Fins and flippers work better than hands and feet in this competition.

The swimming competition

(in approximate maximum speeds)

sailfish—65 mph (105 kph)
bluefin tuna—40 mph (64 kph)
swordfish—35 mph (56 kph)
dolphin—25 mph (40 kph)
whale—20 mph (32 kph)
seeds drifting on the
  Gulf Stream—6 mph (10 kph)
human being swimming—
  5 mph (8 kph)

How about some extra credit for the fancy dolphin jumps, spins, and tail-dancing?

The diving competition

Gannets and boobies dive from a height of 100 feet (30.4 meters) above the ocean's surface.

Special mention for water flying

Diving-petrels use their wings underwater just as they do in the air. They can fly right through waves and even emerge from the water flying.

A LONG MIGRATION

Green turtles are my open-ocean pals, but even I don't know their secrets. How can they find their way from their grazing waters along the coast of South America to their tiny nesting island in the middle of the South Atlantic Ocean? It is one of the world's great mysteries.

You can find green turtles munching turtle grass off the coast of Brazil, near miles of sandy beaches. But when it is time to lay eggs, the 300-pound (136-kilogram) mother turtles turn

When they are not migrating across the open ocean, green turtles cruise above the ocean floor, looking for food. This one was spotted near the coast of Borneo.

away from nearby land and swim 1,400 miles (2,250 kilometers) to tiny Ascension Island, only 5 miles (8 kilometers) long.

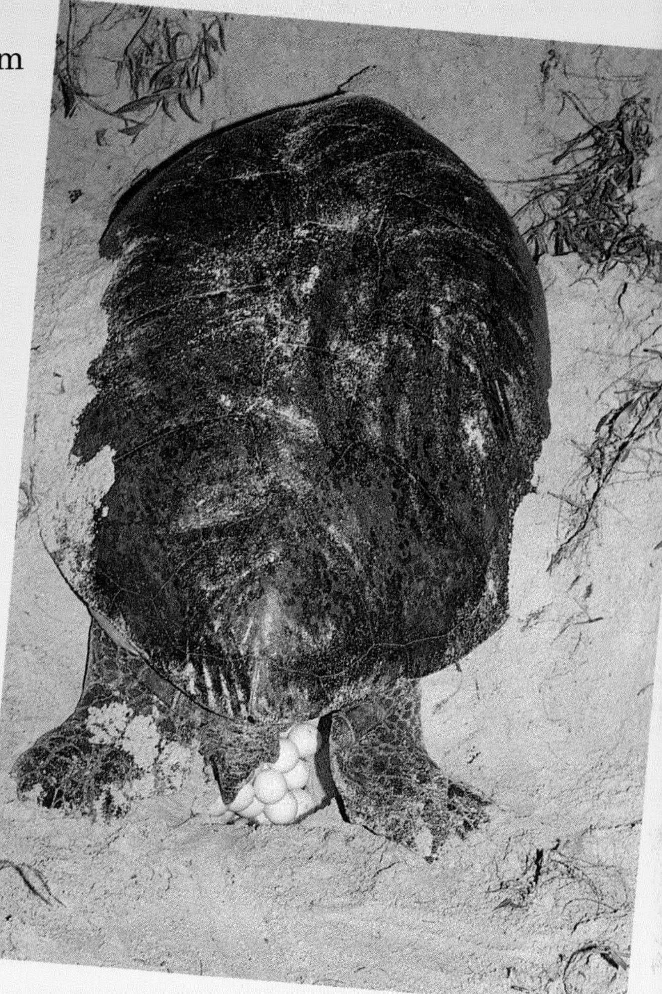

A female green turtle comes ashore only to lay her eggs and bury them on a sandy beach.

Here, each mother turtle lumbers on shore, digs a nest, lays up to 100 eggs, and buries them in the sand. Then she heads back out to the water. In the next few weeks, she comes ashore three to seven times to lay more eggs. Then she starts her long swim home to South America.

Other green turtles make these trips between December and March. Some of them return to nesting grounds in Costa Rica and other spots.

For 50 years or more, starting when they are about 30 years old, the turtles return to the same beaches every two or three years. Mother turtles return to the very beach where they were hatched. But it's hard to imagine why the green turtles return to their "birth beach." Even the eggs are in danger. Dogs, rats, and other animals, including humans, often dig them up.

In six to eight weeks, if the eggs survive to hatch, the baby turtles dig out and "rush" to the water, while birds swoop down on them and lizards, weasels, and other mammals pounce. In the water, fish are waiting for a turtle dinner.

Then, it's into the waves. We don't know where the babies go, but in time, they show up as young adults on the shores of Brazil.

How do the turtles find one beach on a tiny volcanic island so far away? One theory is that baby turtles *imprint* on their birth beach, just as baby salmon imprint on their birth stream. While they are scrambling to the water, the turtles take in clues about their surroundings that help them find their way back years later. Coming back, they may follow their noses. They have a remarkable sense of smell.

Turtle hatchlings dig out of their sandy nest immediately after hatching.

A baby green turtle heads for water. It will survive to reach the sea if predators don't find it first.

Scents, clues in the land and water, and even a built-in "compass" may help this green turtle find its way across the open ocean to its native beach in Hawaii.

They might also use "compasses." Scientists have found that turtles have a *geomagnetic sense*—they can feel the earth's magnetic field. A mineral called *magnetite* in the turtle's brain may work as a compass to help them find their home beach. The constant direction of winds and waves in the South Atlantic Ocean could also help them steer. Maybe they even use the stars to help them steer, as sailors have done.

Possibly, the answer is a combination of all these things. To find such a small island in the vast reaches of the open ocean is an astonishing feat, but somehow green turtles have been finding their tiny island for millions of years.

Dolphins in Peril

Dolphins are among the smartest animals on earth, but for years, many kinds of dolphins were endangered. Luckily, people have stepped in to protect them.

In the 1980's, some fishing crews used huge "drift" nets. These nets, up to 40 miles (64 kilometers) long, trapped every sea creature that came along. The fish that were useful as food were hauled in and taken to market, but thousands of dolphins, along with other fish and marine animals, were dumped back into the sea—dead.

And for years, crews fishing for tuna in the Eastern Pacific Ocean set nets around dolphins to catch the schools of yellowfin tuna that travel with them. The nets made good catches of tuna, but they also killed dolphins.

Many wildlife organizations protested. Finally, the U.S. government and tuna industry leaders made changes. Now, some canned tuna carries "dolphin-safe" on the label. This means the tuna was caught using nets in ways that do not kill dolphins. By international law, a ship that kills too many dolphins loses fishing rights for the rest of the year.

Still, dolphins face many dangers. The United Nations outlawed drift nets in 1992. But the nets are sometimes used illegally, and Fanciscana dolphins are slaughtered for use as shark bait.

Pollution takes its toll, too. Dolphins get tangled in nylon fishing lines, swallow plastic cups and bags, and eat plants and animals filled with chemicals from ships, factories, and harbors. As a result, the dolphins develop serious diseases and die.

People like Bob Schoelkopf and the volunteers at Marine Mammal Stranding Center in Brigantine, N.J., have been saving dolphins, whales, seals, and sea turtles for nearly 20 years.

For example, swimmers found an 8-month-old striped dolphin on a Delaware beach and called the center. Volunteers walked and swam the dolphin around a borrowed swimming pool for days, offering handfuls of fish.

When the baby dolphin was strong enough, it was airlifted to the Miami Seaquarium to live with dolphin foster parents and another 8-month-old baby and to learn some sea skills.

This dolphin died after stranding itself on a sandy beach. An illness may have caused it to lose its sense of direction.

LIFE OF A SAND TIGER SHARK

Do you see that school of bluefish flashing by? Notice that long, slow-moving shadow gliding near it. Now watch what happens. *Wham!* One of those bluefish just became lunch for my neighbor, Ripple.

Ripple is a sand tiger shark. I've known her since she and her brother were born. Like most sharks, they were hatched inside their mother's body, and born alive. Then their mother left them, and they swam off to begin feeding and living on their own.

Ripple was born tough. She began life inside an egg capsule in her mother's womb. There were many other capsules, but Ripple developed first. When she broke out of her egg capsule, she

Rows of narrow, sharp teeth line the mouth of a sand tiger shark, *right*.

Barnacle Bit

The shark is a perfect swimming machine, too sleek and streamlined to go out of style. Fossils show that sharklike fish have been gliding around the ocean for more than 400 million years.

began eating the other capsules that were developing into baby sharks. That food, along with the nourishment she got from her mother's body, made her grow fast. By the time Ripple was born, she was already about 3 feet (1 meter) long. Her brother developed in the same way in another part of their mother's womb, and only the two pups were born.

Like most sharks, Ripple took years to grow up. She was lucky. Many pups die before they are a year old. Even as an adult, Ripple could still become a meal for a great white shark or be caught by someone fishing for sport or food.

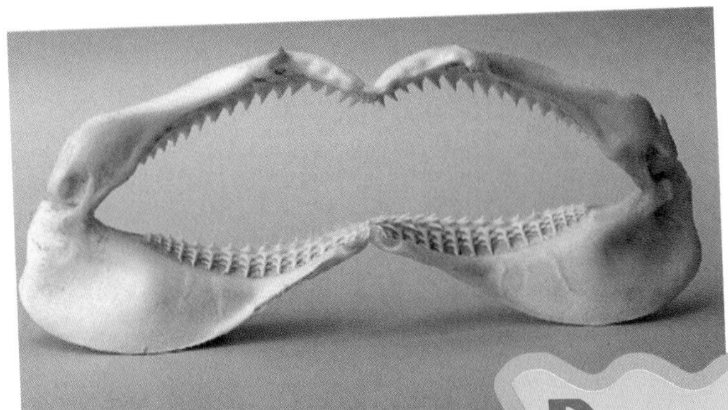

Ripple is now 10 feet (3 meters) long—about as big as she'll get. Like other sharks, she has no hard bones in her body.

Barnacle Bit

Most sharks have 4 to 6 rows of teeth, but they can have as many as 20 rows. They use the outer row till the teeth wear down or fall out, then the teeth behind move forward like fresh troops for the front. A shark can easily use up 2,400 teeth in a year. The tooth fairy would go broke!

Her skeleton is made of tough, flexible cartilage. And although she looks smooth and sleek like me, she is covered with millions of tiny, sharp, hard scales. If you touch her, they can scrape the skin off your hand!

Watch Ripple swim. The long, upper part of her tail fin makes her lift as she moves through the water, and her side fins act like airplane wings. This helps keep her heavy body from sinking. Every now and then she swims to the surface and swallows air. The air in her stomach helps keep her buoyant so that she can "hang" at a certain depth.

Unlike some other sharks, sand tigers don't form schools, so Ripple usually swims alone. Of course, she's a meat-eater. Her meals are smaller, bony fish—bluefish, grouper, alewives, flatfish, mackerel, and even eels—as well as smaller sharks and rays. Her narrow, sharp teeth are not made for tearing or crunching, but they're good for grabbing slippery prey.

See the remoras stuck on Ripple? When Ripple makes a kill, these little fish get the leftovers. To earn their keep, they clean tiny parasites off Ripple, keeping her in shark-shape! Those pilotfish swimming alongside Ripple are hoping for fish scraps, too.

Although she usually hunts alone, Ripple and other sand tiger sharks sometimes find a large school of fish. When that happens, all the sharks circle the fish, driving them into a tight mass. Then the sharks charge in for a banquet.

Sand tigers are medium-sized sharks, and not as ferocious as some of their relatives. But if they are disturbed during mating season or startled by a diver, they're quick to attack. I've seen Ripple chase a diver who tried to take her picture underwater with a flash camera.

When the last mating season came around, Ripple was old enough to mate and have pups. After mating, she and the male shark went their separate ways. While the pups were growing inside her, she stopped feeding. For months, colonies of tiny sea creatures grew all over her sharp teeth, because she wasn't using them! Her pups were born close to the reef, fully developed and ready to swim, just as she had been. Now the pups are on their own, hunting their meals and trying to stay out of danger. As you can see, Ripple is eating again—and her teeth are shiny and clean.

Barnacle Bit

Sharks can detect the faint electric field given off by a fish or a person in the water. They read these signals with special sensors in their heads. Rays and skates also have this ability.

ENTERING THE TWILIGHT ZONE

Welcome to the world just below the sunlit zone. Its dim blue light, colder temperatures, and smaller food supply make for different ways of life.

Do some of these creatures remind you of fireflies? That's not surprising. In the depths of the twilight zone, many living things carry their own light, called *bioluminescence* (BY oh LOO muh NEHS uhns).

In the dimly lit waters below the sunlit zone of the ocean, a viperfish hunts a glowing lanternfish.

A fluorescent comb jelly flashes its bright light in the dark waters of the Arctic Ocean.

WATER WORD

***Bioluminescence* is the ability of living things, such as lightning bugs, fish, and shrimp, to produce light by means of chemicals. Their bodies release an enzyme that makes *luciferin* (loo SIHF ur ihn), a chemical that gives off light. Unlike light bulbs, the bioluminescent spots on an animal don't give off heat.**

Some, such as the lanternfish, flash glowing lights in patterns along their sides—dots of gold, red, blue, green, or pink. Some smaller fish and shrimp use rippling lights along their undersides as camouflage. By copying the wavy patterns of blue light falling through the water, they can't be seen by predators swimming below.

A little farther down, salps and comb jellies use a quick burst of bright light to temporarily blind or surprise an attacker. Copepods blow out glowing clouds to escape from danger.

Look at the ribbonfish drifting in the water. They use a gas-filled float to keep from sinking, in much the same way a Portuguese man-o'-war floats along on the surface.

But even in this dim light, hunters can find a good meal. The viperfish is even scarier than its name. With giant eyes focused up toward the faint light above, a mouth bigger than its body, and long, sharp teeth, this fish is built to catch and gulp down a big dinner.

And then there's the most famous "deep sea monster"—the giant squid—gliding around the twilight zone at depths of 3,300 feet (1,000 meters). Never captured alive or in one piece, the squid is believed to grow more than 50 feet (15.2 meters) long, tentacles and all.

Of course, the sperm whale, who loves to dine on squid, also cruises the twilight zone. The world's deepest diving mammal, the 60-foot (18-meter) sperm whale has been reported at depths as great as 8,000 feet (2,400 meters).

But you don't have to dive this far down to see a light show. Every night, creatures from the twilight zone, including squid and shrimp, migrate up to the surface waters of the open ocean to hunt small fish and graze on plankton.

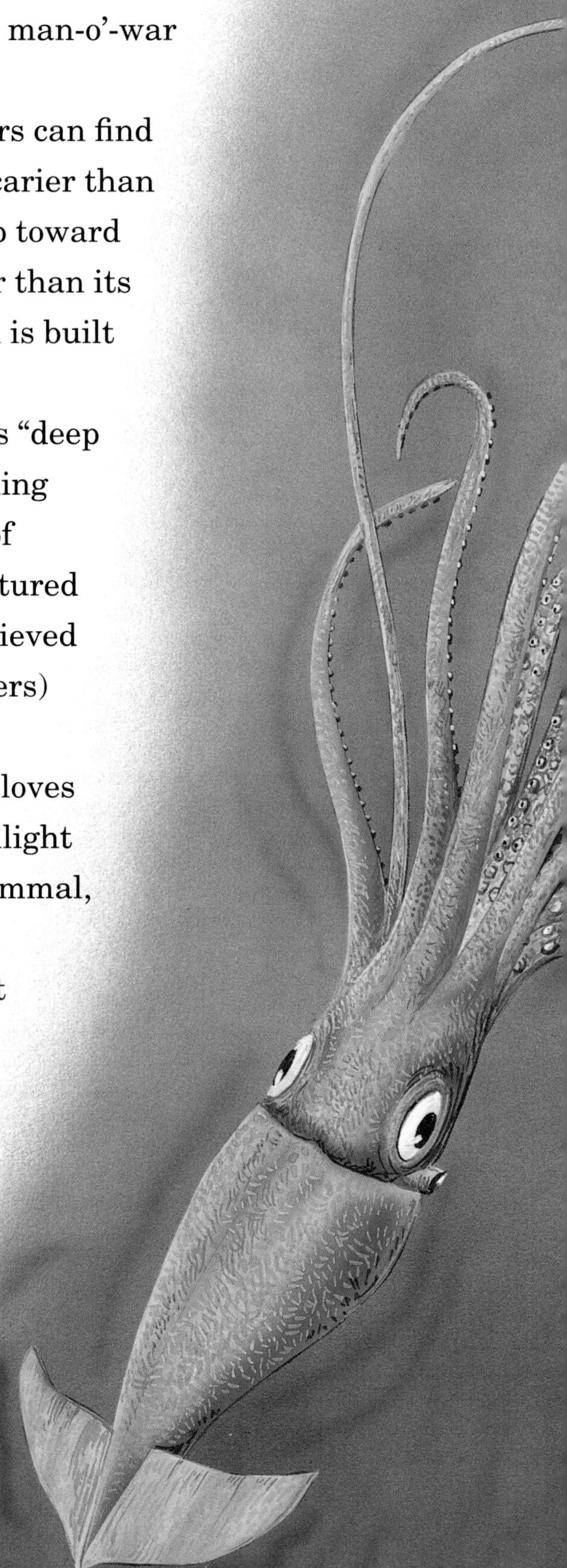

Believe me, it can take you by surprise! Imagine seeing hundreds of brightly lit squids leaping right out of the water all around you. Sailors have reported glowing squids and rare deep-sea snakes jumping into their boats.

Barnacle Bit

Scientists have learned about giant squid by examining dead or dying specimens that were washed up on shore, dragged in by fishing crews, or found in the stomachs of whales. They also have learned by examining sucker marks that scientists believe squid have made on whales.

OCEAN PEAKS

Don't be fooled by the calm and level surface of the ocean. There's a lot going on down below. Take a look!

The first thing you notice is that the ocean floor is moving! You didn't know that? Don't feel bad. Scientists didn't really understand it until about 40 years ago.

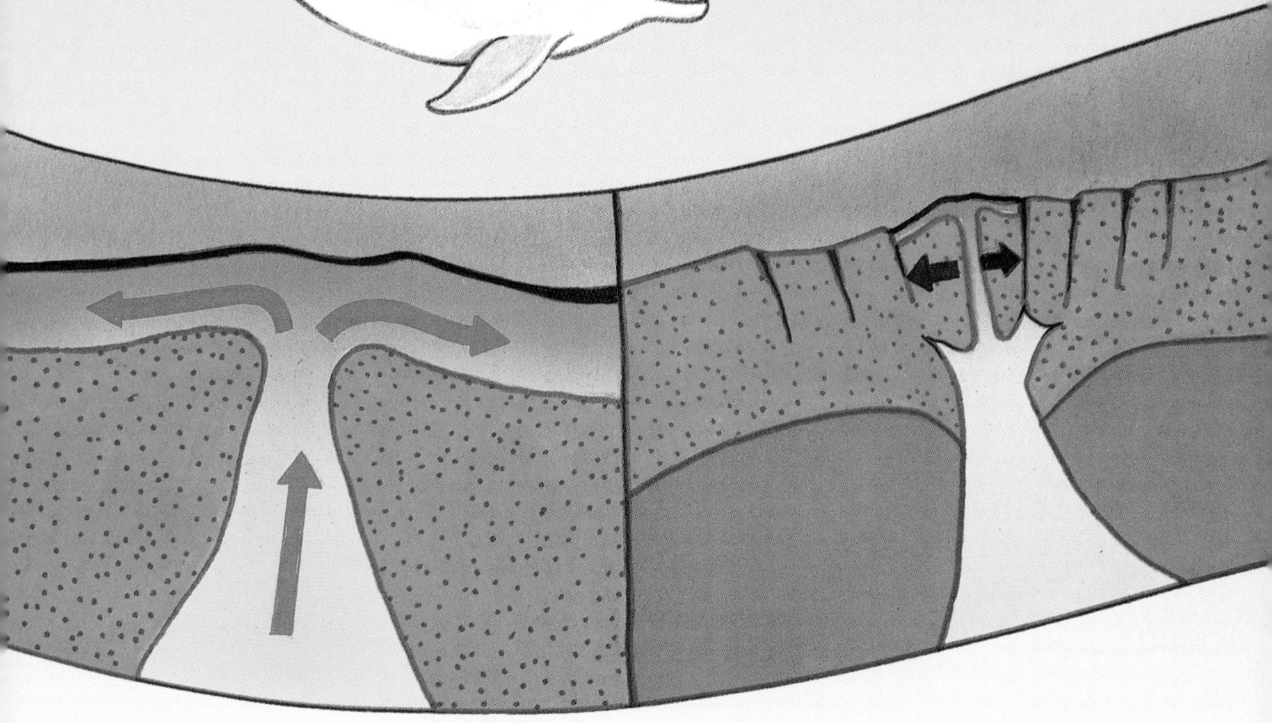

The sea floor begins to spread when hot molten rock called magma pushes up through cracks in the earth.

As it rises to the cool water, the magma hardens into ridges, pushing apart the ocean floor.

All the continents started out 200 million years ago as one supercontinent, then slowly drifted apart. Here's what's happening. On the ocean floor, hot molten rock called magma from inside the earth pushes up through cracks, forming volcanic mountain ranges and continually adding new material. These cracks measure from 8 to 30 miles (13 to 48 kilometers) wide and 1 mile (1.6 kilometers) deep. As the magma cools, it hardens into ridges, pushing the center of the ocean floor apart to make room.

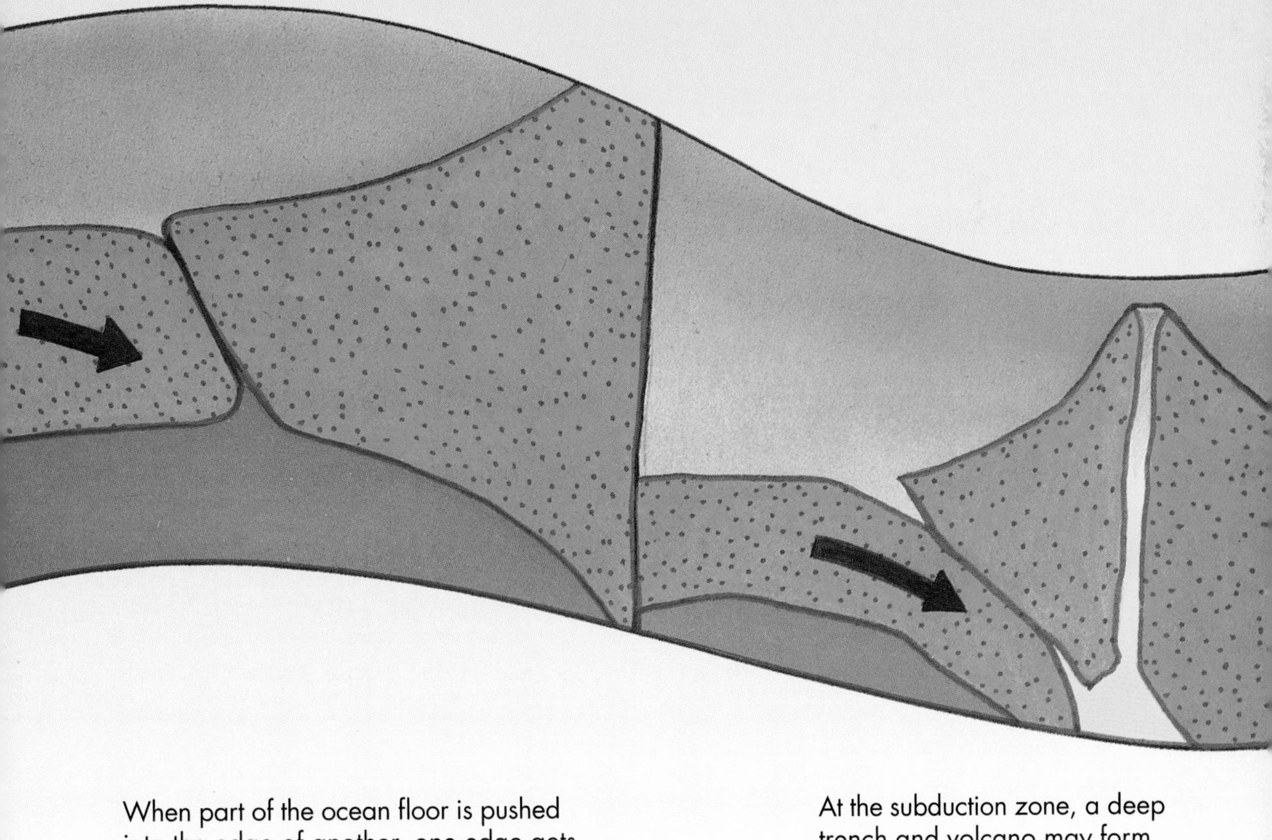

When part of the ocean floor is pushed into the edge of another, one edge gets forced down under the other.

At the subduction zone, a deep trench and volcano may form.

When part of the ocean floor hits the edge of a continent, or another part of the ocean floor, it is forced down. At the *subduction zone,* where the floor slides under, it forms deep trenches and volcanoes. The edge of some of the "old" ocean floor is forced back down inside the earth to be recycled as magma again.

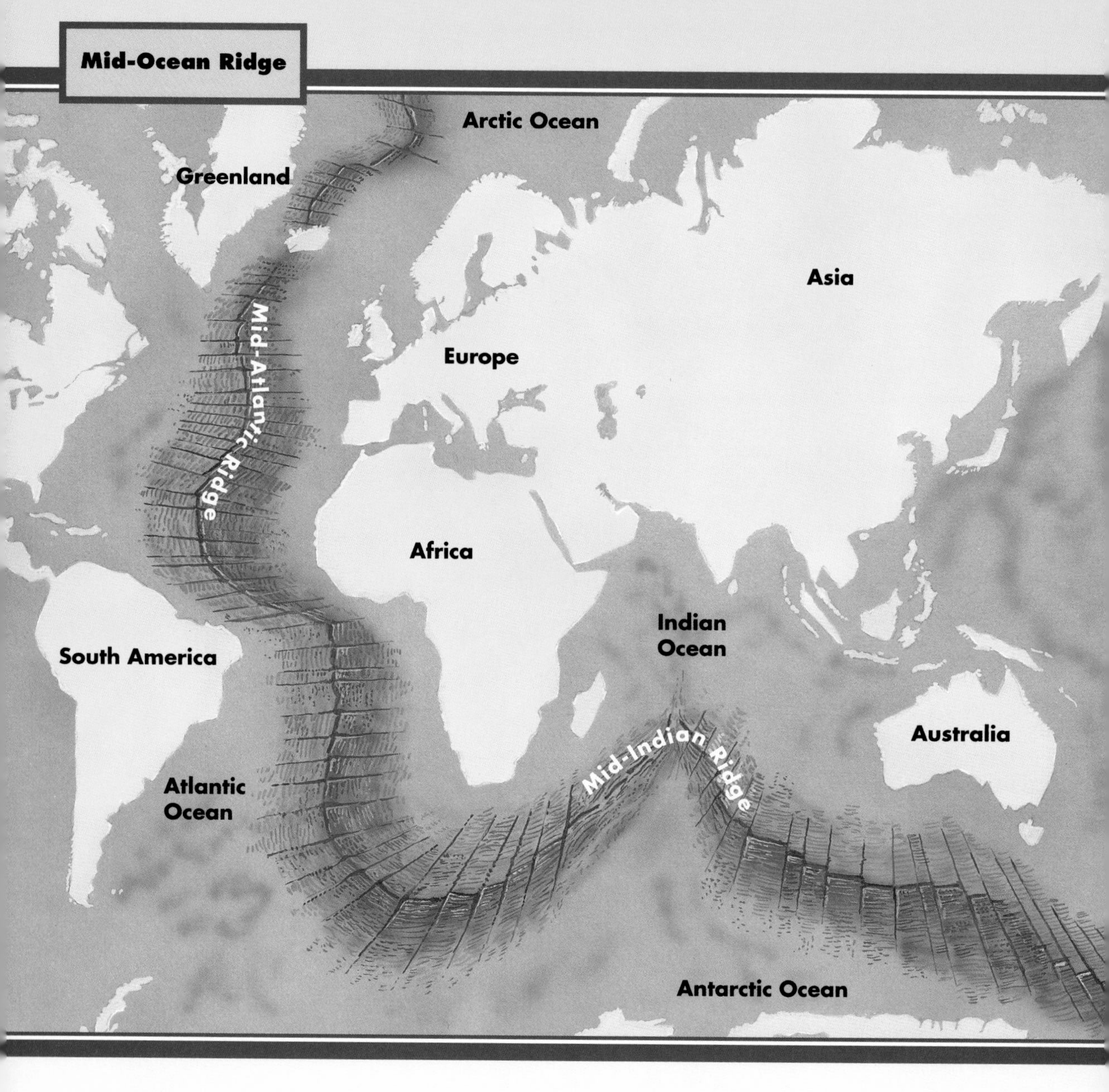

The ocean floor spreads only about 2 inches (5 centimeters) per year, but look where the ocean floor slides under the continents if you want to find earthquakes! The volcanic mountain range under the middle of the ocean is the biggest single feature on the planet. Put your finger on a map of the Mid-Ocean Ridge, then follow the ridge around from the Arctic, Atlantic, Indian, Antarctic, and Pacific oceans. That's about 37,000 miles (60,000 kilometers) of mountain range! It's called the Mid-Atlantic Ridge in the Atlantic, the Mid-Indian Ridge in the Indian Ocean, and the East Pacific Rise in the Pacific.

Many of the little islands scattered around the wide oceans are actually the tops of underwater mountain ranges. In the Pacific Ocean, you'll see underwater volcanoes. In some places you'll see the flat, pointed, or cone-shaped tops of underwater mountains called *seamounts.* The highest seamount is the Great Meteor, 13,123 feet (4,000 meters) high and more than 62 miles (100 kilometers) wide at its base.

Oops, looks like these waters are too deep for me. But you go on. Have fun and be sure to stop by on your way back to the surface.

THE DEEP

Hi! I'm Flash, a lanternfish, and it's my job to introduce you to the world of the Deep. That's where I live. I know most of the neighborhood pretty well, and it's lots of fun. You'll explore some fabulous places—from hot vents to trenches. And you'll meet ocean explorers who have helped us learn about the Deep.

WHAT WE KNOW ABOUT THE DEEP

The world we call "the Deep" is a place of inky darkness, where no plants can grow.

Scientists divide the Deep into three zones. The *bathyal* (BATH ee yuhl) *zone* starts at approximately 3,300 feet (1,000 meters) and goes down to about 13,100 feet (4,000 meters).

The *abyssal* (uh BIHS uhl) *zone* is about 13,100 to 19,700 feet (4,000 to 6,000 meters) below the ocean surface.

And the deepest depths lie in trenches at the *hadal* (HAY duhl) *zone*—from 19,700 feet to more than 36,000 feet (6,000 to 11,000 meters).

Because there are no plants, food in the Deep is scarce. Many creatures there feed on the remains of once-living things and other wastes that sink from waters nearer the surface. Other creatures feed on one another.

The colossal weight of thousands of feet of water makes the pressure greater than most living things can stand. But underwater vehicles called *submersibles* have carried explorers to the Deep. Submersibles are smaller than submarines but can travel much deeper.

Sea level

Bathyal zone

Abyssal zone

Abyssal plain

Hadal zone

Most of the deep ocean bottom is a vast, flat expanse called the *abyssal plain.* Reddish-brown clay or a mixture of plankton skeletons called *ooze* covers most of the sea floor.

It's also cold down in the Deep, usually only a few degrees above freezing.

DWELLERS OF THE DEEP

My neighbors deep down in the sea include some of the weirdest, scariest-looking fish you'll ever want to meet. Some have gaping mouths, some have teeth like daggers, and some have colored spots that glow in the dark with the

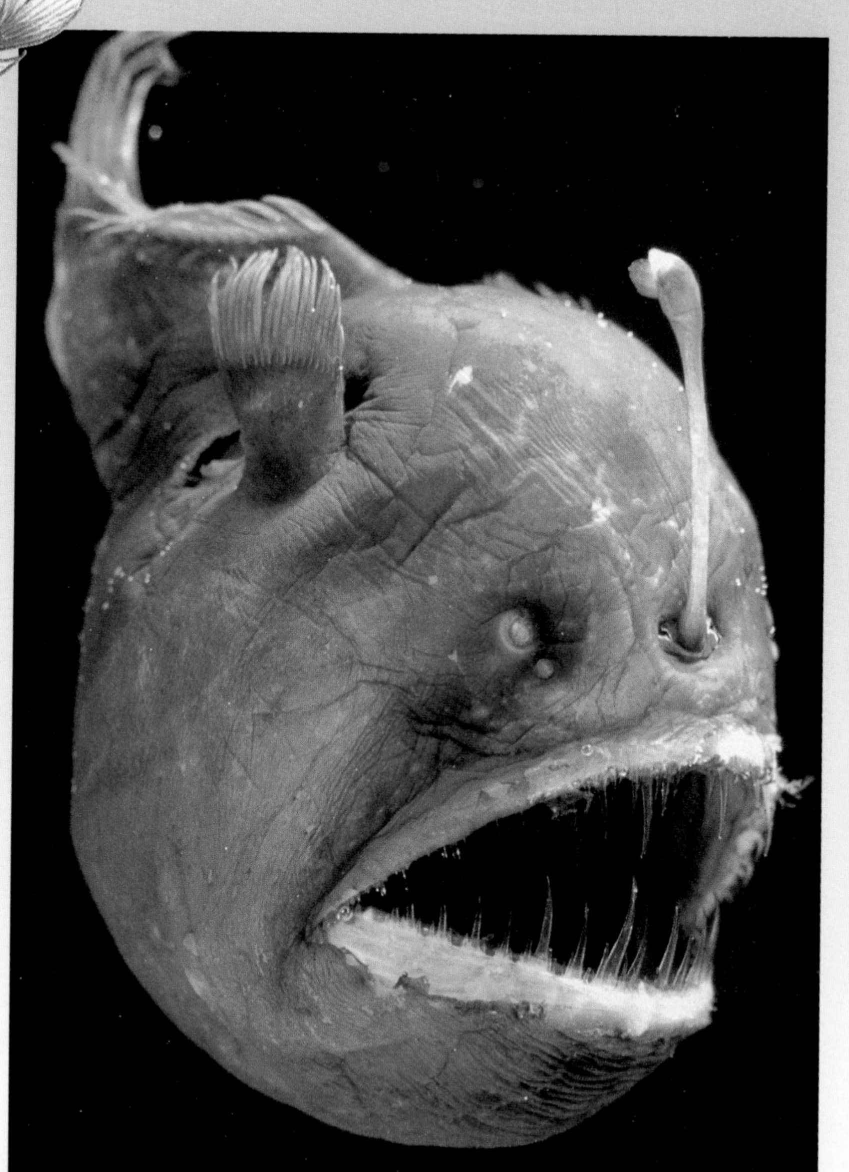

Hanging motionless, an anglerfish waits for a smaller fish to approach the "bait" above its mouth.

light of bioluminescence (remember that glow that some fish have?). Most of us are just a few inches long, and even the big ones are rarely more than a few feet.

Try to remember that deep-sea fish look weird for a good reason. We're all specially designed to live in the harsh conditions of the Deep. Since food is scarce, we have developed all sorts of ways to get a decent meal. We also have ways of protecting ourselves from all the creatures that want to gobble us up.

Take anglerfish, for instance. They are small fish that spend most of their lives hanging motionless in the water. They get their food by "fishing" for it with a "fishing rod" that grows out of the fin at the back of their head. The glowing blob at the end of the rod acts as a lure. When a curious or hungry fish approaches, thinking the glowing lure may be a tasty morsel, the anglerfish gobbles the creature down.

With our huge mouths and stretchable stomachs, many of us deep-sea fish are able to eat creatures larger than ourselves. After all, we never know when we'll be getting our next meal.

Barnacle Bit

One reason it is difficult to study deep-sea fish is because they don't usually survive being brought up to the surface. Many deep-sea fish brought up in nets die because of the sudden temperature change. Others arrive on deck with their *swim bladder* bursting. A swim bladder is a gas-filled organ that some fish have to help them float. When the water pressure on a deep-sea fish decreases, the gas in its swim bladder expands.

The gulper eel is among the largest deep-sea fish, up to 2 feet (61 centimeters) long, and one of the champion big mouths. It seems to be all mouth and stomach.

Many kinds of fish are specially colored to protect them from predators. Hatchet fish are round, flat, and shiny like a coin. Their silvery bodies are lighter on the bottom so that they blend in with the dimly lit waters above, making it hard for predators to see them. Their jutting lower jaws make them look like they're pouting, and their eyes point upward, possibly to make it easier for them to see their food.

We lanternfish are among the travelers of the Deep. Every night, many kinds of lanternfish swim to the surface to feed on plankton and other tiny creatures. Many of us have multicolored lights along our bellies. Like the coloring of the hatchet fish, these spots make it harder for predators to see us from below. The lights are also used to attract mates. And some of us have glowing spots under our eyes—headlights that help us see in the dim water.

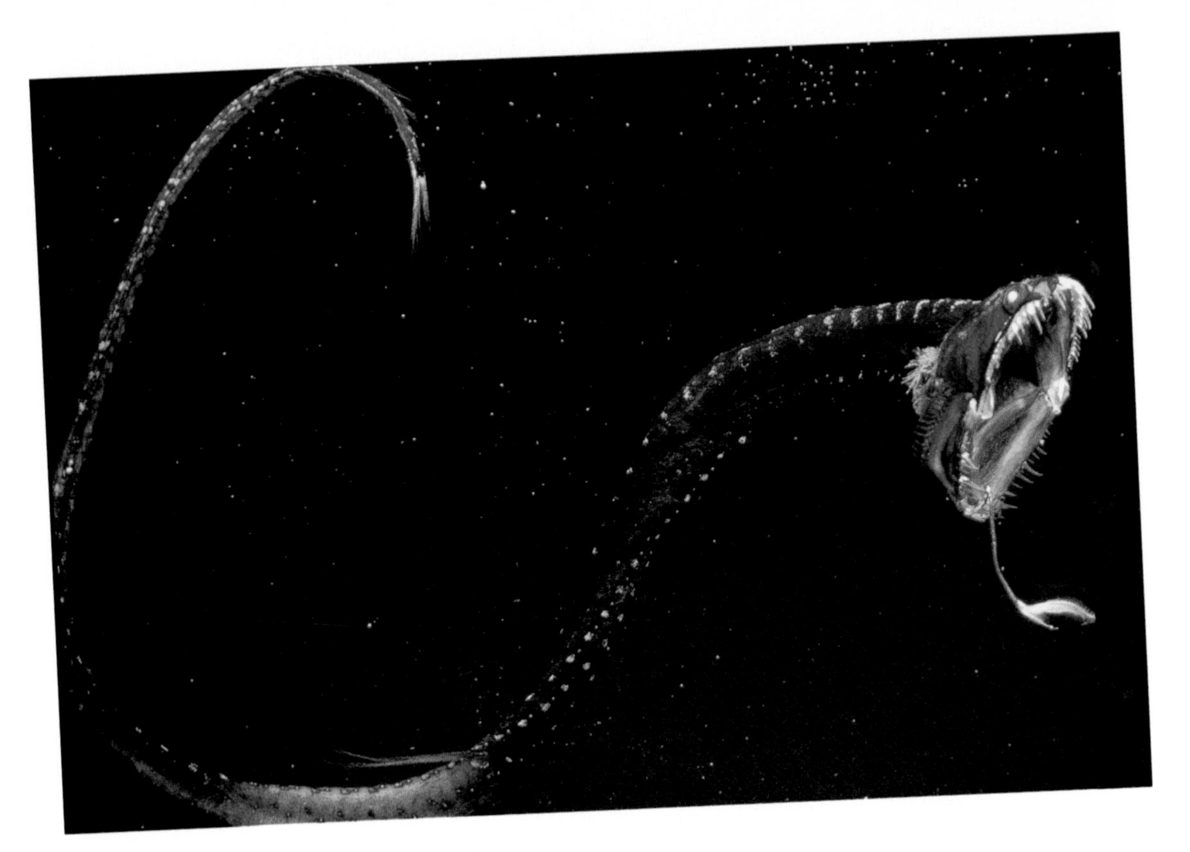

A dragonfish dangles a "bait" that grows from its lower jaw to attract its prey.

We lanternfish have to be careful at all times. There are so many fish down here that could gobble us up in an instant. Dragonfish are scary stalkers. Like the anglerfish, dragonfish use a "fishing pole" to attract prey. But the dragonfish's pole hangs from its lower jaw.

Fish aren't the only creatures living down here. The sea floor is strewn with brittle stars that crawl in the mud and worms that burrow there. Bright red shrimp and bioluminescent squid glide along in the darkness. And jellyfish in rainbow colors trap other deep-sea creatures with their stinging, clinging tentacles.

Scientists believe the Deep supports many other forms of life that no one has ever seen. Only time—and further exploration—will reveal them.

S E A L A B

Make Your Own Hot Vent

Build a mini-oceanarium and hot vent to see what happens in the Deep.

Things You Need:

- *small, plastic bottle and scissors; or modeling clay*
- *aluminum foil*
- *small baby-food jar*
- *large, clear pitcher or jar (the taller the better)*
- *2 pots or pitchers*
- *red food coloring*
- *long, dull knife*

1. Take the cap off the plastic bottle. Have an adult help you cut off a piece of the top big enough to fit over the small jar. Or shape a hot vent out of clay.

2. Fill the pots with cold water. Set aside.

3. Fill the small jar with hot water. Add red food coloring.

4. Working quickly, cover the jar with foil and place it on the bottom of the clear pitcher under your plastic or clay vent.

5. Pour cool water into your mini-oceanarium until it reaches well above the top of the vent. Then use the knife to open the foil completely. Watch what happens.

Is some water redder than the rest? As in your mini-oceanarium, hot fluids rise from ocean hot vents. Try the experiment using only cold water. Compare the results.

"GARDENS" IN THE DARK

Though plants can't grow in the dark Deep, colorful "gardens" of other organisms do. Red-tipped worms more than 5 feet (1.5 meters) long sway in the current. Pale crabs pick their way over carpets of colored bacteria. Blue-eyed pink fish called eelpouts swim among beds of white clams and yellow mussels up to 12 inches (30 centimeters) wide. And animals called siphonophores (SY fahn uh fors) look like dandelion puffs hanging above the ocean floor.

This is the world of underwater hot springs called *hydrothermal vents.* The first hydrothermal vents were discovered in 1977 off the coast of South America in the Pacific Ocean, at a depth of about 9,200 feet (2,800 meters). Until then, scientists never dreamed that so many kinds of large animals could thrive in such lightless depths.

Hydrothermal vents form along the oceanic ridge, where hot, partially melted rock rises to the earth's surface. As the young rock cools, it cracks, and seawater seeps into these crevices. As the seawater comes into contact with the melted rock, the water becomes tremendously hot and dissolves minerals out of the surrounding rock. Soon, the hot water begins to rise back up through the rock and escapes through openings in the sea floor. The cold seawater from above cools the hot water coming from below, making the dissolved minerals solid again. These solid

Barnacle Bit

One of the largest known black smokers lies off the northwest coast of Washington state. It's about 160 feet (48 meters) high and still growing. If you were asked to name a black smoker like that, what would you call it? The scientists who discovered this one named it after the smoke- and fire-breathing star of many Japanese sci-fi movies—Godzilla!

minerals form chimneys. Water darkened by the mineral sulfur escapes from the chimneys, giving the vents their nickname "black smokers."

While most life on earth gets its energy from the sun, the gardens of the hot vents grow by using energy from the dissolved minerals that spew out of the vents. Bacteria growing around the vents use the mineral sulfur to create food without light. This process is called *chemosynthesis* (KEE moh SIHN thuh sihs). Some animals around the vents feed on the bacteria. Others feed on the bacteria-fed animals.

Tube worms from the deep ocean can be many feet long. Dr. Robert Ballard and an assistant hold one found off the Galapagos Islands.

At first, vent worms called *Riftia* puzzled scientists. How did they eat with no mouth, stomach, or guts? Researchers discovered that the same bacteria that grow around the vents live in the worms' bodies. The worms absorb sulfur from the seawater, and the blood vessels that give *Riftia* its bright red "head" carry the sulfur to the bacteria in its body. The bacteria use the sulfur to make food.

Scientists believe that the hydrothermal vents may provide clues about how life on earth began. Researchers have discovered that many vent creatures match fossils which are hundreds of millions of years old. Some scientists believe bacteria that use chemosynthesis may have been the first living things on earth billions of years ago.

IN THE TRENCHES

The deepest part of the ocean floor lies in the hadal zone, in the steep-sided ocean trenches. Here the water can be almost 7 miles (11 kilometers) deep.

Scientists only know, so far, of some marine creatures living in the crushing pressure and darkness of the trenches. For example, certain species of sea anemones attach themselves to the rocky walls. Others live in the mud at the bottom along with bristled polychaete (PAHL ee keet) worms. Mouthless, gutless beard worms there absorb food directly from the seawater.

BARNACLE BIT

If you could put the world's highest mountain—the 29,028-foot (8,848-meter) Mount Everest—in the deepest known point in the ocean, Challenger Deep, there would still be more than 1 mile (1.6 kilometers) of water above the mountaintop.

Shelled animals also live at great depths. But the minerals that make up the hard shells of sea creatures dissolve under such heavy water pressure. As a result, those in the hadal zone have fragile shells.

One of the most interesting trench creatures is the *pycnogonid* (PIHK nah guhn uhd). Pycnogonids, also called sea spiders, may have four to eight long legs, each measuring more than 10 inches (25 centimeters).

A sea spider stalks across the ocean floor on legs many times longer than its body.

Giant, thin-shelled clams cluster in a trench off the Galapagos Islands.

BRAVING THE DEEP

It's hard to think of an underwater challenge that Dr. Sylvia Earle hasn't taken on. She has spent more than 6,000 hours—or a total of 250 days—underwater and on one occasion lived there for two weeks. She was the first person to reach the bottom of Crater Lake in Oregon—about 1,500 feet (457 meters) down—and among the first to travel 3,000 feet (914 meters) under the ocean in a one-person submersible. She has even discovered new species of sea creatures and algae—some have been named after her. She has escaped an attacking shark and has survived the sting of a poisonous lionfish.

Dr. Earle was the first woman appointed chief scientist at the National Ocean and Atmospheric Administration of the United States. And she helped start a company, called Deep Ocean Engineering, that designs and builds submersibles.

But Earle is probably best known as the holder of the record for the deepest dive without a *tether* to the surface. When people dive very deep, they wear a special pressurized suit that looks somewhat like an astronaut's space suit. Usually, they are also tied, or tethered, to a boat at the surface. A dive such as Earle's was incredibly dangerous because it would have been almost impossible to save her if anything went wrong.

Earle's dive took place in 1979, off the coast of Hawaii. Wearing a protective "Jim suit," she rode to the bottom of the sea strapped to the front of a submarine. At the bottom, 1,250 feet (381 meters) down, Earle unhooked herself from the sub, leaving only an

18-foot (5.5-meter) tether connecting her to it. She spent the next 2 1/2 hours strolling along the ocean floor, which was partially lighted by the sub's headlight. She watched fish swim by with their lights flashing and examined bioluminescent coral that glowed when she touched it.

Although Earle's explorations have brought her fame—and the nickname, "Her Royal Deepness"—she is more concerned with studying the sea and telling people about what she has experienced there, so that people may become more concerned about protecting its natural treasures.

Dr. Sylvia Earle's company has been working on a submersible that can fly like an airplane 4,000 feet (1,219 meters) below the ocean's surface. One day her submersible, *Deep Flight,* may allow scientists to travel easily and quickly under the sea and observe things no one has yet seen.

Dr. Sylvia Earle, deep ocean specialist

SECRETS OF THE TITANIC

April 15, 1912, was the date of one of the world's most tragic sea disasters. Hours before dawn that day, the *Titanic,* a British luxury liner on its first voyage, sank in the North Atlantic Ocean after hitting an iceberg. About 1,500 people died in the freezing water. For the next 73 years, the ship lay unseen but not forgotten, 12,500 feet (3,800 meters) down in the jet-black depths.

This picture shows the *Titanic* before her only voyage in April 1912.

Dr. Robert Ballard, an American ocean scientist and explorer, first began to dream of finding the wreck of the *Titanic* in 1973. It took him twelve years to raise money for the project and design a craft that would help him locate the lost ship. Finally, Dr. Ballard was able to set up an expedition with a group of French and American scientists.

The search began in late June 1985, during the short North Atlantic summer. The search team had only five weeks before the weather would turn bad.

For days, the ship *Knorr* towed *Argo,* a sledlike machine with a video camera, back and forth over the ocean floor in the area where the searchers thought the *Titanic* would be. But for more than two weeks the team saw nothing. Ballard's spirits sank. Then suddenly, after midnight with only a few days left in the mission, *Argo* beamed back pictures of something that looked like part of a ship. A hush fell over the searchers as everyone watched the screen. Finally, a hazy round object came into view. It

An artist's illustration shows how the *Titanic* looked when it was explored 73 years later by a robot, *Jason Junior.*

was one of the *Titanic's* boilers, the huge coal-heated steam tanks that powered the ship.

Everyone on board rejoiced. They had found the *Titanic*.

Over the next few days, *Argo* and a machine called *Angus* sent back pictures. What the searchers found down there after examining photographs and videos, was both astonishing and sad. The *Titanic* had broken in half. The front part of the ship was upright but driven partway into the mud on the ocean floor.

Then, too soon, it was time for the trip to end. When the explorers got back home, the world already knew of their discovery. Ballard was a hero.

In 1986, Ballard and other searchers went down in the submersible *Alvin* to see the wreck for themselves. They made ten dives in *Alvin,* taking hundreds of photos and hours of videotape. They also took Ballard's remote-controlled robot *Jason Junior* along to explore places that were too small or dangerous for *Alvin* to go.

Barnacle Bit

In 1987, researchers aboard the submersible *Alvin* discovered communities of creatures similar to those around the hydrothermal vents. However, these creatures clustered around the body of a dead whale 4,000 feet (1,200 meters) below the ocean surface. In this case, sulfur from the decaying whale—not a vent—fed bacteria that supported the community.

At the site, they found that the back part of the ship was about 2,000 feet (609 meters) away from the front. A field of wreckage—bed frames, sinks, broken windows, tea cups, wine bottles, and even the head of a doll—lay scattered in between.

The ship showed the wear and tear of its seventy-three years in the deep. Oozing sheets of rust, which Ballard named "rusticles," covered

A whole teacup, *below,* lies in the debris scattered from the sunken ship.

Giant "rusticles"—icicles of rust—hang from the steel bow of the *Titanic, left.*

the metal ship. Masts were broken, and the big smokestacks called funnels were missing. But many windows were still intact. Ballard also saw the crow's nest, the steel arms from which the ship's lifeboats were lowered long ago, and the bronze steering telemotor from the wheelhouse.

Ballard was most anxious to get a look at the oaken Grand Staircases, two of the ship's most beautiful features. Down into an opening in the ship's deck went *Jason Junior,* which acted as the explorer's "eyes" as it moved around the ship. But hungry sea creatures—wood-boring mollusks—had long since eaten away nearly all of the wood on the ship. Almost nothing of the staircase remained.

A photograph shows one of the magnificent Grand Staircases on the *Titanic.* Most of the wood had been eaten away by the time the wreck was found.

In this illustration, the artist shows the submersible *Alvin* resting atop the *Titanic* while *Jason Junior* explores inside the ship.

In 1987, a French team returned to the *Titanic* to collect objects from the wreck. Ballard believed strongly that the ship should be left untouched, so he took no part in the project. The French team brought up many valuables, including china, silver, and even a safe filled with jewelry, coins, and paper money. Many such artifacts from the wreck, along with photos, are now part of a *Titanic* exhibit at the National Maritime Museum in Greenwich, England.

Do You Know the Deep?

After reading this chapter with a friend, have fun testing your memory.

Things you need:

- ***pencil***
- ***paper***
- ***5 kinds of coins or buttons for each player***

How to play:

1. Draw a grid—3 squares across and 3 squares down.

2. Decide who will be the first player. Then the other player asks that person question #1. If the player answers correctly, he or she gets to put a marker on any space on the grid, and the turn passes to the other person.

3. If the player answers incorrectly, no markers are placed, and the turn passes to the other person.

4. The winner is the first person to fill a row up, down, across, or diagonally.

1. What is another name for hydrothermal vents?

hot vents, black smokers, hot springs

2. Why don't plants grow in the Deep?

There isn't any sunlight there.

3. What is one way fish use bioluminescence?

to make it harder for other fish to see them; to light their way in the dark; to attract prey; to find a mate

4. Who discovered the wreck of the *Titanic*?

Dr. Robert Ballard

5. Scientists divide the Deep into what zones?

bathyal, abyssal, hadal

6. What is ooze?

the cover of plankton skeletons on the sea floor

7. What is the Challenger Deep?

the deepest known point on the ocean floor

8. What is chemosynthesis?

the process used by bacteria at hydrothermal vents to make food out of the mineral sulfur (instead of out of sunlight)

9. What is the deepest zone of the ocean called?

the hadal zone

10. What happened on April 15, 1912?

The Titanic sank.

11. What was the name of the robot that explored the wreck of the *Titanic*?

Jason Junior

12. What is bioluminescence?

the ability of animals to produce light with chemicals inside their bodies

13. What is *Alvin*?

a submersible

14. What is the abyssal plain?

the flat expanse that covers most of the bottom of the sea

15. Name one animal that lives around hydrothermal vents.

white clams, yellow mussels, Riftia, eelpouts, siphonophores

16. Where are hydrothermal vents usually found?

on the ocean floor where melted rock escapes to create new sea floor

17. Who is Dr. Sylvia Earle?

the woman who holds the record for the world's deepest dive not tethered to the surface, also known as "Her Royal Deepness"

18. How was the wreck of the *Titanic* found?

with an underwater camera called Argo attached to the Knorr; Argo was sent about 12,500 feet (3,800 meters) down

19. Near what part of the ocean are most trenches located?

near the continents

20. How do beard worms eat?

by absorbing food directly from seawater

POLAR OCEANS

People often lump the Arctic and Antarctic together, calling them the "polar regions." After all, both are icy, and bitter cold during their long winters. But take it from me, they are very different. I'm Slippery, a seal, your guide to the northernmost and southernmost parts of the ocean. Throw on a parka and follow me.

THE COLD FACTS

The Arctic and the Antarctic may look alike at first glance, but they are actually poles apart—literally.

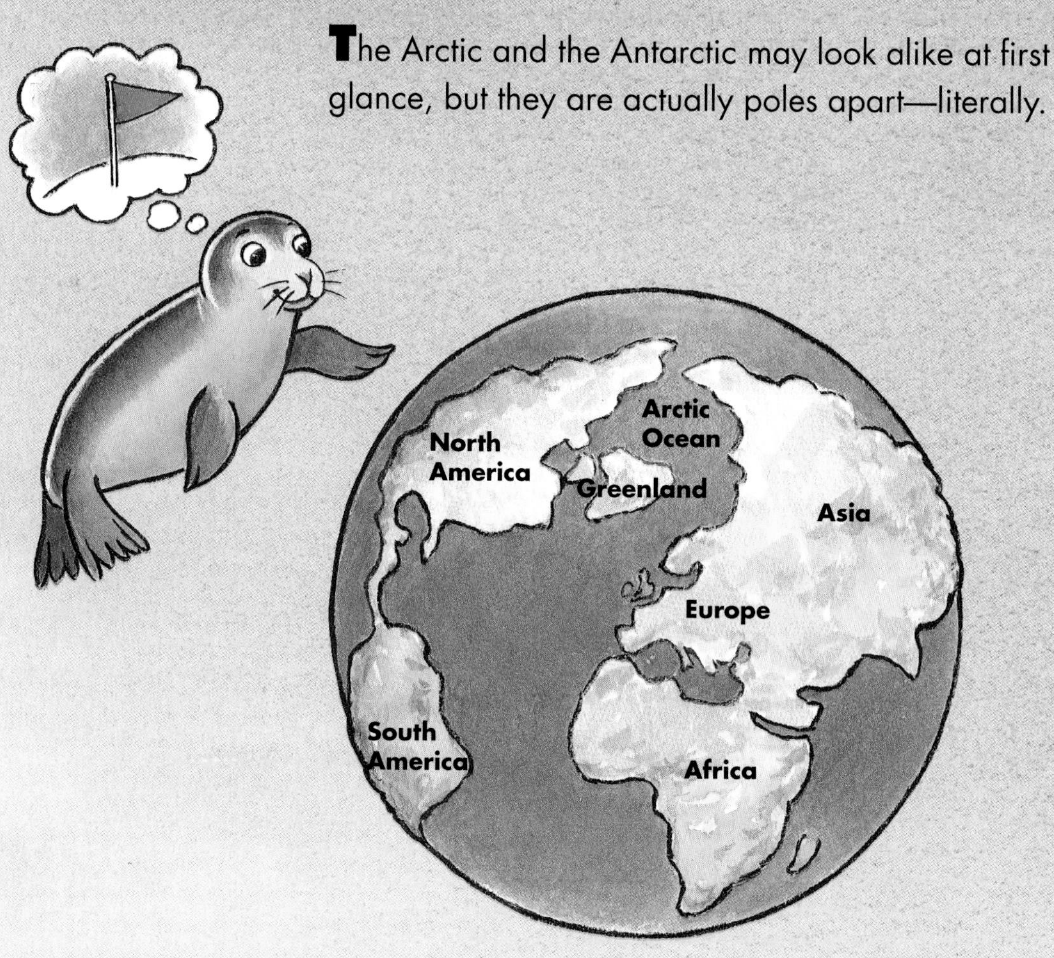

The North Pole is not located on land, as you might think. It is in the ice-covered part of the Arctic Ocean. The Arctic Ocean is surrounded by the northernmost parts of Europe, Asia, and North America and by many islands, including Greenland.

The South Pole also is in an icy place. But this ice is an *icecap* that covers the continent of Antarctica. The ocean around Antarctica is sometimes called the Southern Ocean or the Antarctic Ocean.

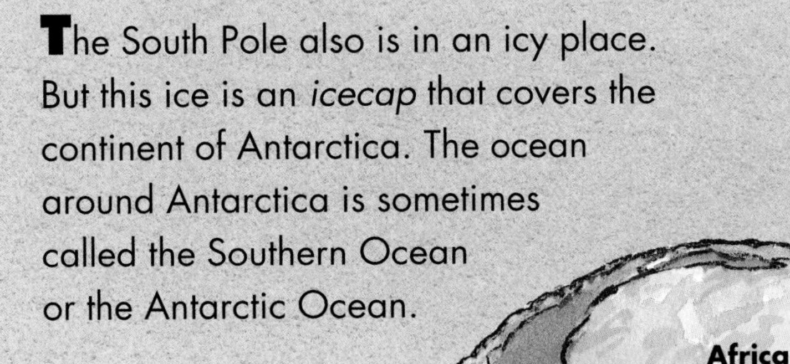

The ice that covers the Arctic Ocean is frozen seawater. This "sea ice" averages about 6 1/2 feet (2 meters) deep. The ice that covers Antarctica is made of frozen snow. This "snow-ice" has built up over millions of years to a thickness of 15,700 feet (4,800 meters)—almost 3 miles (5 kilometers)—at its densest place.

Icebergs in the polar regions differ, too. Most Arctic icebergs form when masses of ice break off from glaciers on Greenland. These icebergs look like jagged peaks rising 400 feet (120 meters) out of the ocean. These are only the tips, however. Up to nine-tenths of the berg lies below the surface.

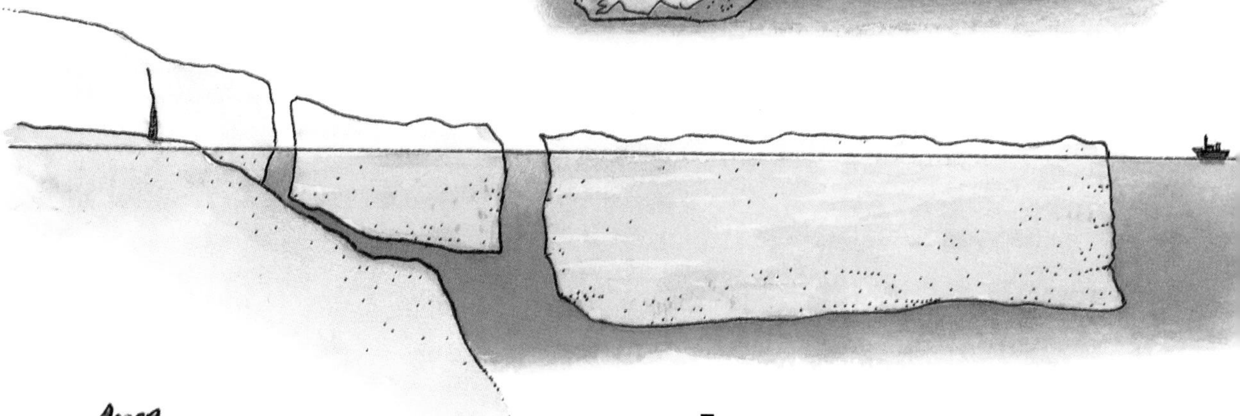

In the Antarctic, icebergs form when huge, flat chunks of sea ice break loose. Antarctic icebergs have flat tops and sometimes measure up to 200 miles (320 kilometers) across.

The polar oceans are alike in some ways. Compared to the polar air temperatures, the water is warm! Except for the layer close to the frozen top, the water usually stays around 30 °F (-1 °C)—a lot warmer than the air on ice or land. Central Antarctica, for example, has had air temperatures as low as –128 °F (–89 °C). As a result, many animals live in or near the water.

Only since the mid-1900's have people, mainly researchers, regularly inhabited Antarctica.

However, the Arctic has been inhabited for thousands of years by Arctic peoples, including North American Inuit, European Lapps, and other groups.

Certain kinds of birds and mammals, such as seals like me, thrive in Arctic and Antarctic waters. Feathers, fur, and fat conserve our body heat. And the ocean supplies plenty of food, such as shrimplike Antarctic krill. Mmm—very tasty!

ICE-ING ON THE ARCTIC CAKE

Do you like sliding on ice? Good! Let's visit the Arctic. The ice there is amazing.

The Arctic has two basic types of sea ice: *pack ice* and *fast ice*. Pack ice covers most of the ocean. And fast ice freezes fast—or firmly—to the shores of land surrounding the ocean.

Both kinds of ice start out the same way. First, ice crystals form as the ocean cools in the winter. The crystals float on the surface, making a gray slush called *grease* or *slob ice*.

Barnacle Bit

Salt drains from the top layer of first-year ice during the spring. This creates *candle ice*. Candle ice is so fragile that it shatters with the touch of a fin or a gust of wind, making a sound like the tinkling of glass wind chimes.

Next, the grease ice merges into thin, bendable sheets. Waves and wind make these sheets of ice collide and they form thicker, rounded sheets called *pancake ice*. As the pancakes collide, their edges rise and thicken. Eventually they freeze together and form an ice cover.

When sea ice becomes *opaque* (oh PAYK)—so thick that it looks white and you can't see through it—it's known as *first-year ice*. By spring, first-year ice is 6 to 7 feet (1.8 to 2 meters) thick. If it doesn't melt during the summer, it becomes *multiyear ice*. By this time, the hard freeze has

Constant collisions and grinding caused by wind and waves have turned thin sheets of ice into these rounded pieces of pancake ice.

driven the salt out of the top layer of the sea ice, and ice crystals have taken the salt's place. The crystals give multiyear ice a bluish color. *Blue ice* is a good source of fresh water for drinking. After several years, pack ice grows about 10 to 12 feet (3 to 3.7 meters) thick.

Multiyear ice makes up much of the pack-ice cover. Remember how it began as pancake-shaped ice with raised edges? In summer, the ocean under the ice eats away at these edges, creating deep crevices. Arctic visitors—human and otherwise—have to watch out or they might fall through a crack!

An ice floe is a resting place for walruses on Baffin Island in the Canadian Arctic.

The pack ice at the edge of the ice cover seldom grows thicker than 6 1/2 feet (2 meters). Winds, waves, and water currents keep this ice constantly moving and prevent it from forming a solid covering. Instead, it forms *floes* (flohz)—huge sheets of floating ice. Ice floes measure many miles across and often crash together, creating ridges called ice *hummocks.* These hummocks, sometimes as high as a two-story building, get in the way of people trying to cross the pack ice.

The only smooth ice in the Arctic is the fast ice that forms between the shore and the pack ice. In winter, the fast ice extends far out to sea, and people sled across it easily.

Ice is important for life in the Arctic. The ice keeps the ocean's heat from escaping into the air, so the water stays warm enough for plankton to multiply and for fish to swim. And the Arctic mammals, such as polar bears and walruses, hunt, sun, and even sleep on the ice.

WATER WORD

In summer, the ice floes often break apart, creating *leads* (leeds), or stretches of open water. When winter comes, the leads freeze over with thin *young ice.* Travelers over the ice pack recognize young ice by its dark color, and they proceed with caution.

Pulling a load over ice hummocks is hard work, even for experienced sled dogs and drivers.

ANIMALS OF THE ARCTIC

Few animals live in the middle of the Arctic Ocean. The heavy cover of pack ice shuts out light. Phytoplankton—the plankton that use sunlight to make food—can't survive there. So animals that feed on these plankton can't live there either. But the edges of the ocean get more sunlight and are much livelier. Plankton and fish thrive there, even under ice. Let's dive in and do some fish-watching.

Sculpin

Snailfish

The fish in the Arctic are strong swimmers—they move through cold water, which is denser than warm water. That spiny-headed, warty-skinned fish is a sculpin. Sculpins have huge appetites. They often snack on zooplankton, and they even steal fishing bait. Arctic fishers eat them, though sculpins are just full of bones.

Do you see that pink snailfish? Snailfish come in many colors, such as purple-brown, red-orange, and light brown. They're clever too—

they hide their eggs in crabs' gills. There, the eggs are protected from predators and get the oxygen they need to survive.

Do you see that big furry hulk over there? It's a polar bear—my worst enemy! The average polar bear catches about 50 seals a year. Sometimes a bear stands guard above a breathing hole waiting for a swimming seal to pop up for air. It even covers its black nose with its white paws to blend in better with the ice. Other times the bear sneaks up on a seal that's swimming, or sleeping, or sunning—and pounces!

Barnacle Bit

Arctic zooplankton include some strange animals. There are sea gooseberries, which use many rows of *cilia* (hairs) to move around; shrimp that give off light to help them recognize one another in deep, dark water; and sea butterflies, which have shells and fleshy "wings" that they use to swim.

Polar bears swim so well that some scientists classify them as marine mammals. When a polar bear catches a seal, it usually eats only the fatty blubber. Blubber provides more energy than the protein in seal meat, so unless a bear is really hungry, it leaves the meat. When there are not enough seals, polar bears go after mice, lemmings, salmon—even birds' eggs and beluga whales. How does a polar bear hunt a whale? It attacks the whale's blowhole to disable the huge creature. In summer, polar bears add berries and other plants to their diet.

Barnacle Bit

Hunting and pollution have taken their toll on the polar bear population. In response, five countries with land in the Arctic agreed in 1973 to limit the hunting of polar bears, and Russia and Norway have totally banned it. Some countries allow Arctic peoples who rely mainly on polar bears for food to hunt a small number of bears in traditional ways.

It's lunchtime. Those beluga whales out there are probably looking for a tasty bite. They like cod, squid, herring, halibut, flounder, and shellfish. But young whales don't hunt for their dinner. They drink their mother's milk, which contains more than ten times as much fat as cow's milk.

The belugas must be on the move. Listen to them trilling and whistling to guide the herd along. That's why they're called "sea canaries." A beluga whale has an oil-filled lump on its head that scientists believe helps it buzz, grunt, bang, and click. Scientists think the clicks may help belugas navigate and locate food.

Like many other whales, white beluga whales travel and feed in groups. Brownish river waters pouring into Hudson Bay, Canada, make these belugas appear gold.

Oh, no! Here comes a polar bear looking for lunch. I better get going. See you later!

LIFE ON THE POLYNYAS

Welcome to an oasis in the Arctic—the great North Water Polynya. A *polynya* (puh LIHN yuh) is an area of open water surrounded by sea ice and found in the same region year after year. Some polynyas, such as the North Water, are ice-free the year around. Others freeze over in the winter months but open in March or April.

Polynyas cover only a small part of the Arctic Ocean. The North Water, the largest, covers about 30,000 to 40,000 square miles (75,000 to 100,000 square kilometers). A small polynya near Baffin Island is just 197 to 295 feet (60 to 90 meters) across. But the importance of polynyas is great.

Ivory gulls and walruses are regular visitors to the open waters of Arctic polynyas. For some kinds of seals, polynyas are a permanent home.

Like a green oasis in a hot, dry desert, the open water of a polynya surrounded by ice teems with life. Shellfish and fish graze on phytoplankton. Sea birds come to breed, to stay all winter, or to feed on their way north each spring. Seals, walruses, beluga whales, narwhals, and polar bears visit polynyas, and Inuit come to hunt.

WATER WORD

Polynya **comes from a Russian word meaning "an open field" or "a clearing in the forest." Russian explorers thought it an appropriate name for these clearings in the Arctic ice. The Antarctic has polynyas, too, but they attract fewer kinds of animals than Arctic polynyas.**

When summer is over, the polynya population decreases. Many birds migrate south for the winter. Most whales and walruses migrate to the open sea. But ringed and bearded seals stay the year around.

In the past, the Inuit also lived and hunted near polynyas. A Canadian archaeologist has uncovered the remains of Inuit settlements near polynyas in the Far North. The archaeologist believes that people lived in these settlements for thousands of years.

Why do the waters in a polynya stay ice-free year after year while the surrounding sea freezes? Scientists think wind is important. In some places, it blows sea ice away as fast as it forms. Winds from over Greenland, for example, keep the North Water open. Upwelling is also important. In some areas, deeper, warmer water moves up to the surface and prevents freezing. Fast currents also help create polynyas because rapidly moving water cannot freeze.

This polynya looks heavenly. Dive in!

Barnacle Bit

In 1964, a change in wind patterns closed a polynya near Cape Bathurst in the Canadian Arctic. As a result, about 100,000 eider ducks could not find food to eat or open water to settle on. Starved and exhausted, the birds died on the ice.

Create Your Own Currents

What causes some currents? Do this activity and find out.

Things you need:

- *a large, clear plastic storage box*
- *a large jar or pitcher*
- *blue food coloring*
- *an ice-cube tray*
- *ground pepper*

1. Fill the jar with water. Add food coloring and stir to make the water dark blue.

2. Fill the ice-cube tray with the blue water. Put it in the freezer overnight.

3. The next day, pour warm water into the storage box until it is half full. Sprinkle pepper on the water to help you see motion on the surface.

4. Place a colored ice cube at each end of the box. Watch the ice melt. What do you see?

Cold water is heavier than warm water. So, as the ice cubes melt, the cold water sinks down and flows along the bottom. It creates a cold current.

In the ocean, cold polar water also sinks, and warmer water rises to the top. This creates currents that mix the layers of water and spread food, oxygen, and salt more evenly through the ocean.

ANIMALS OF
THE ANTARCTIC

Antarctica is my idea of a vacation paradise. Every summer, several kinds of seals and penguins come here to breed, raise their pups, and hunt. Compared to other coasts around the world, Antarctica looks deserted. But take a peek below the surface of the ocean—just a few feet down—and you'll find a different kettle of fish altogether.

Krill

In spring and summer, the Antarctic Ocean teems with *krill.* These shrimplike creatures form swarms that look like red patches near the surface. Krill are food for many animals in the Antarctic Ocean.

Just look at the crowd down here! There are all kinds of unusual Antarctic fish, including shiny cod icefish and striped crocodile icefish. Did you know that icefish have clear blood? They look almost transparent. And like other Antarctic fish, icefish make their own "antifreeze." It's a natural substance in their blood that keeps them from freezing.

Barnacle Bit

Icefish have only one-tenth as much oxygen in their blood as other fish have. But they have larger hearts, larger blood vessels, and more blood than other fish. And they move very slowly, so they don't need as much oxygen when they swim.

The liveliest place in the Antarctic is the ocean floor. Many Antarctic fish lay their eggs there to protect them from the ice on the surface. The eggs and newborns are especially large to help them survive in the harsh environment. Certain kinds of crabs, worms, sponges, mollusks, sea stars, and sea anemones also live on the ocean floor. They can withstand much lower temperatures than their tropical cousins.

Cold Antarctic waters, rich in krill, support icefish and other sea life. Sponges, sea stars, anemones, and brittle stars flourish on the ocean floor.

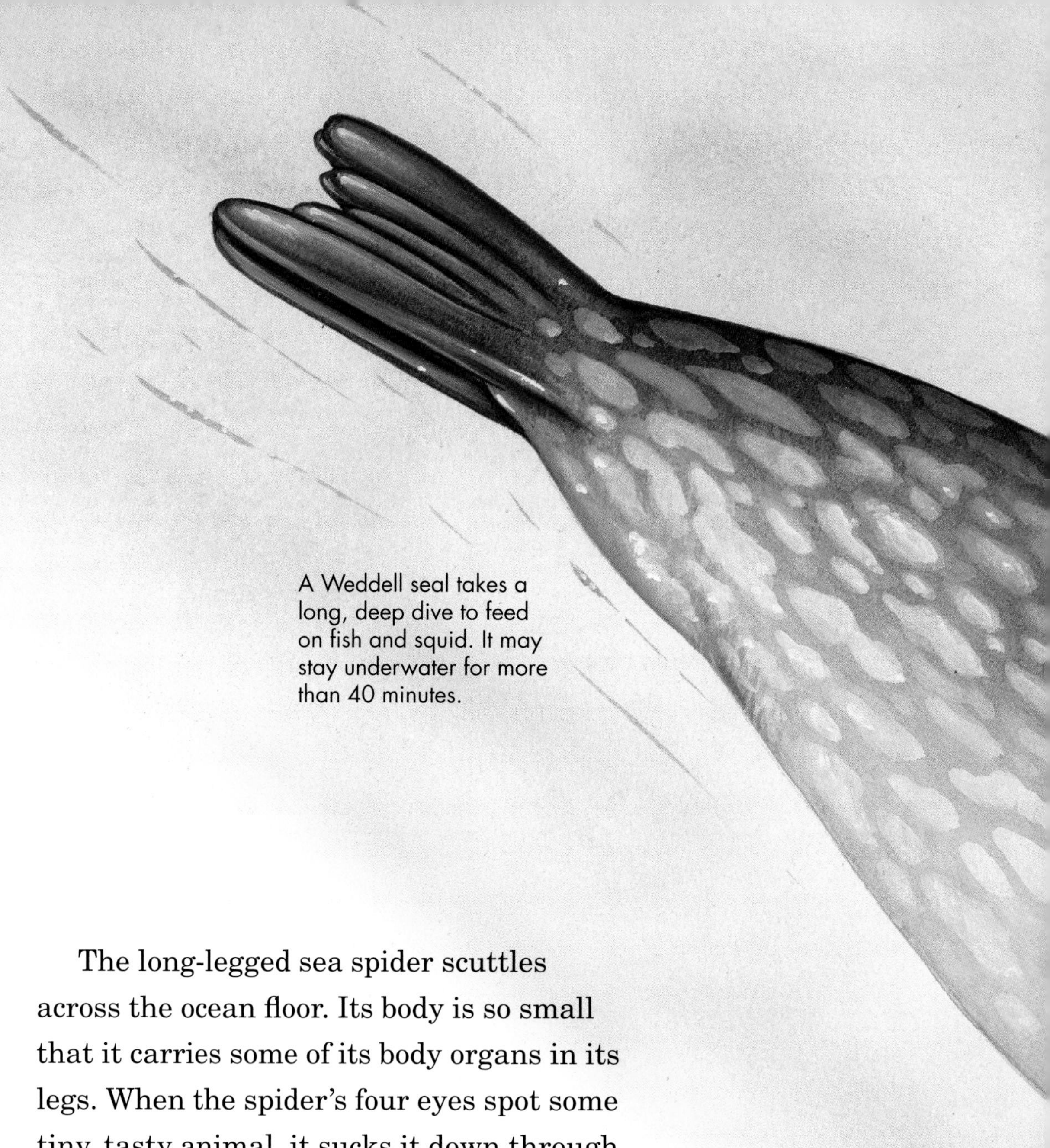

A Weddell seal takes a long, deep dive to feed on fish and squid. It may stay underwater for more than 40 minutes.

The long-legged sea spider scuttles across the ocean floor. Its body is so small that it carries some of its body organs in its legs. When the spider's four eyes spot some tiny, tasty animal, it sucks it down through its proboscis—remember, that's its built-in eating tube!

Many whales—fin, blue, minke, right, sei, and humpback—travel to the Antarctic each spring and summer to eat their fill of krill. In addition, orcas, also known as killer whales, come south, looking for seals, squid, and other treats.

At least six different kinds of seals live in the Antarctic at some time of year. The most numerous are crabeater seals. These seals don't really eat crabs. They strain krill out of the water with their interlocking teeth.

Weddell seals are known as the world's most southerly mammals. They stay in the Antarctic the year around and spend the entire winter in the water feeding on fish and squid. They dive as deep as 2,360 feet (719 meters) and they can stay underwater for more than 40 minutes. Even I can't hold my breath that long!

BIRDS OF THE POLAR REGIONS

In the Arctic, spring is truly bird-iful. Sea birds come to the Arctic shores every year to nest and raise their young.

The brownish-black-and-white bird over there is a common murre. Murres have colonies on high cliffs, but they do not build nests. They lay single, pear-shaped eggs on bare rock ledges. When the eggs move, they roll in a circle rather than off the ledges.

Some people call the tufted puffin the "sea parrot." That's because this bird has a blond cowlick and a brightly colored bill. In the Arctic, puffins nest in rock crevices or in tunnels that they dig with their beaks and feet.

Arctic people look for the arrival of king eider ducks, which are as big as geese. In each colony, tens of thousands of ducks line their nests with soft down feathers and hatch their young. After the young leave the nests, people gather the down to stuff pillows, mattresses, and coats.

BARNACLE BIT

Murre eggs come in colors from white to bluish-green with red, brown, or black markings. Parent birds identify their eggs by these colors and markings.

This pair of eider ducks has returned to summer nesting grounds on Ellesmere Island, Canada, to raise young.

The Polar Inuit also eagerly await the coming of the dovekies in May and June. In fact, their word for May means "the month when the dovekies return." They consider raw dovekies a great delicacy. Dovekies scoop up zooplankton with their small, round beaks. These stocky little birds have black heads and bright white undersides.

That high-flying bird is an Arctic tern. In summer, the tern comes here to mate and to hatch its chicks. When winter approaches, it takes off to enjoy summer in the Antarctic.

Then, during the Antarctic winter, the tern returns—a round trip of more than 20,000 miles (32,000 kilometers) each year.

Arctic tern

Let's follow the Arctic tern to Antarctica. All penguins live in the Southern Hemisphere, but only Adélies, chinstraps, emperors, gentoos, and king penguins come to Antarctica to breed. Emperor penguins lay their eggs on the ice but never go on the land.

An emperor couple produces only one egg each winter. Shortly after the female lays it, the egg is transferred to her mate's feet. He covers it with his loose skin to keep it warm.

Barnacle Bit

You thought you saw a tern crying? No, you probably just saw liquid salt dripping off the tern's beak—not tears! A gland above a sea bird's eyes removes salt from food and water and then allows the salt to run off the bird's beak.

Then the female leaves to look for food because she has not eaten for two months. When the temperatures drop, the males huddle together to keep themselves and the eggs warm. After two months, the females return and the eggs hatch.

An Adélie penguin, *right,* watches as a scientist measures and marks its egg.

A colony of gentoo penguins, *left,* gathers on a rocky peninsula in Antarctica.

Penguin eggs need protection from the cold, but the greatest danger to the young comes from predatory birds. Skuas fly over penguin colonies, swooping down on eggs and chicks. Luckily, even a small penguin can chase a skua away. Pigeonlike land birds called sheathbills also snatch penguin eggs. Sheathbills hop about, looking for eggs and anything else they can eat. They even steal the krill that parent penguins chew and spit out for their chicks.

Adult penguins have no enemies on land. But leopard seals and even killer whales lurch out of the water to grab the birds off the ice. I'd hate to worry about being a killer whale's dinner. Wouldn't you?

Skua

Adélie penguin

Barnacle Bit

Skeletons of penguins' ancestors show that they once measured perhaps 5 1/2 feet (1.7 meters)—quite a bit taller than the 4-foot (1.2-meter) emperor, which is the largest kind of penguin in the world today.

TOO WARM OR **NOT TOO WARM?**

Should I dress to stay warm or to keep cool? Who knows? All around us, scientists find signs that the earth's climate is getting warmer, but they cannot tell whether it will stay warm or get cooler again.

The facts keep coming in. The world's average temperatures are reported to be about 1 Fahrenheit degree (0.6 Celsius degree) higher than those in the late 1800's.

Temperatures on parts of the Antarctic coast have increased even more—as much as 4.5 Fahrenheit degrees (2.5 Celsius degrees) since the 1940's. In the past 25 years, three Antarctic ice shelves have broken up into flocks of huge icebergs as much as 45 miles (72 kilometers) across—that's the length of approximately 660 football

Typically, the earth's atmosphere allows some heat from the sun to reflect from earth and escape back into outer space. But when certain chemicals are released into the earth's atmosphere, they make the atmosphere act like a greenhouse, *right.* Then the atmosphere traps more heat from the sun and reflects it back to the earth.

fields! Scientists think that the breakup of the ice was caused by the rise in temperatures there.

Why have temperatures on the earth risen? In part, because automobiles, factories, and furnaces have been pouring carbon dioxide and other gases into our atmosphere for years. Scientists and environmentalists agree that these gases cause a *greenhouse effect*. The gases trap heat next to the earth, raising temperatures, much like the glass or plastic walls of a greenhouse do.

BARNACLE BIT

Antarctica's icecap contains nine-tenths of all the ice on the earth.

However, whether the earth's overall climate will continue to get warmer or begin to get cooler is not clear. In many parts of the world, the weather changes from year to year. These changes may be caused by a number of factors relating to the air, land, and ocean. So it takes many years of measurements to discover even slight changes in the overall climate of the earth.

Some scientists predict that world temperatures will continue to rise—approximately 3.6 to 9 Fahrenheit degrees (2 to 5 Celsius degrees) by the year 2050. They also claim that this *global warming* will melt the ice at both poles. Such a massive meltdown would cause the oceans to rise 10 feet (3 meters) or more, flooding islands and coastal areas around the world.

However, scientists Anne de Vernal of Quebec and Eugene Domack of New York think global warming will bring different results. By studying layers of sediment from the floors of the polar oceans, they discovered that polar ice was building up thousands of years ago. And, at that time, the land and oceans were *warmer* than they are today.

So, why was the ice growing instead of melting in that warm climate? The warmer temperatures of the ocean surface caused more water to evaporate. Winds carried this moisture over the land and dropped it as snow. But not much snow

Some scientists think that continued global warming will melt the polar ice and cause the world ocean to rise.

Other scientists predict that global warming will cause more snow to fall, bringing colder weather, more frozen ocean water, and a new ice age.

melted in the Arctic and Antarctic because temperatures there were still very low. This made the polar ice increase, even though the earth was getting warmer.

De Vernal has suggested that the greenhouse effect and global warming could bring on another ice age. The growing polar ice would reflect more sunlight back into space, and the earth would absorb less of the sun's warmth—cooling the climate even more. Then sea levels would be lower—not higher—because so much ocean water would be ice.

Whichever way the world goes—hot or cold—the process will take a very long time. So don't worry about your wardrobe just yet.

A World Laboratory

During the International Geophysical Year (IGY), from 1957 to 1958, Antarctica became a symbol of world cooperation. *Geophysics* includes the study of the earth and its atmosphere and waters. During the IGY, 12 nations set up research bases on Antarctica and nearby islands. And almost 100 people spent the winter in the heart of Antarctica.

The IGY researchers used Antarctica as a huge laboratory. *Meteorologists*—scientists who study the weather—sent up balloons several times a day to measure wind, moisture, pressure, and temperature. *Glaciologists*—scientists who study glaciers—drilled holes 1,000 feet (305 meters) deep to obtain ice cores. They examined the cores—their layers, gases, and more—to find out how Antarctica's climate and atmosphere had changed over the years.

Since the IGY, many countries have agreed to use Antarctica—which was not claimed by any one nation—only for peaceful purposes, and to allow scientific investigation to continue freely. Scientists study the atmosphere, the ocean, glaciers, and other features that tell them about the earth's health. In fact, they consider Antarctica the ideal place to study changes in the climate and in the *ozone layer.*

Ozone is a special form of oxygen found high in the earth's atmosphere. It absorbs heat from the sun. It also acts as a powerful shield, protecting plant and animal life on land and in the water from the sun's harmful rays.

Scientists have discovered that large holes in the ozone

layer appear over the Antarctic each spring. They believe that chemicals polluting the air make the holes increase. By constantly measuring the levels of ozone in the Antarctic atmosphere, scientists can tell whether the holes are growing or shrinking.

In addition to the ozone, environmentalists and scientists also worry about fuel spills and the dangers they hold for Antarctica's wildlife. A supply ship from Argentina, the *Bahía Paraíso,* ran aground on the Antarctic Peninsula in 1989 and leaked at least 160,000 gallons (605,650 liters) of diesel and jet fuel. The fuel covered the surrounding waters. Many penguins, seals, and sea birds died as a result.

The world community is trying to prevent further damage to the polar environment. Many countries established rules that forbid mining in Antarctica for 50 years. And with the help of the IGY, important research to preserve the world environment continues.

A scientist studies Antarctic ice.

WORLD OCEAN

Briny's my name. I'm a swordfish. Don't let my beak scare you. I only thrash it around when I'm under attack, and you look friendly. Speaking of attack, sometimes I think our world ocean is under attack. Careless fishing crews, dirty water, garbage—all big problems in the big blue. Maybe you can help. Read on.

THE OCEAN'S SYSTEM

Just look at the ocean view—so much life all around. Yet I have seen many changes taking place—some harmful to marine life. Many times, the ocean's system can deal with temporary changes, but long-lasting or frequent ones can mean trouble.

For example, a violent storm may wipe out an entire kelp forest. But, given time, the forest will naturally rebuild itself. In addition, crews sometimes overfish an area, leaving only a few small fish to reproduce. But if fishing is limited, the fish will be able to reproduce and increase their numbers again.

Wetlands help trap and break down many wastes that run off the land. The soil in wetlands filters wastes from run-off water, and the plants and animals get nutrients and minerals from the wastes. By the time run-off water reaches the ocean, many of the wastes have been removed.

On the other hand, if global warming causes violent storms to continue and if crews continue to carelessly overfish, marine life may never get the chance to recover.

Pollution poses more problems. Sometimes businesses and homes along the shore dump wastes in the ocean. Also, sewage from far inland—where people might not think about the ocean—travels down streams and rivers, eventually ending up in the sea. Fertilizer and even used motor oil find their way into the water.

In some cases, swamps and other wetlands can filter out wastes that run off the land. Certain nutrients and minerals are used by the plants and animals in a swamp. Other waste particles combine with sediment around roots and soil. In addition, waves and currents can help wash away wastes before they have a chance to build up and wipe out an entire

BARNACLE BIT

When heavy blasting was used off Newfoundland to deepen a channel, many whales, including older, experienced ones, were caught in fishing nets. Scientists believe the loud noise interfered with the whales' ability to find their way by using sound.

marine community. Unfortunately, people have continued to pollute the ocean. They have also taken over much of the coastline for farms, houses, and resorts, removing the protective wetlands.

Why worry about losing marine life and ruining ocean habitats? It is important not to lose living things because *biodiversity* (BY oh duh VEHR suh tee) helps keep the community alive. Biodiversity is the variety of living things in a community. *Bio* means "life," and *diversity* means "difference" or "variety." The greater the number of different species living in a system, such as the ocean, the greater the biodiversity of the system.

The greater the biodiversity of a system, the better its chances for survival. That is, if there are many kinds of plants and animals in an area when a disease or disaster hits, there is a better chance that some kinds of plants or animls will survive. But if there is only one kind of kelp growing in an area when a disease or disaster hits, the entire community could be without food if that one type of kelp does not survive.

Protecting marine life is also important because in a system such as the ocean, all living things

The more kinds of marine life in a community, the greater the biodiversity, *top*. However, if pollution or overfishing causes the number of species to decrease or fade, *middle*, eventually only a few, if any, species will remain, *bottom*.

depend on each other—and we all depend on the ocean. For example, whales naturally die and then sink to the bottom of the ocean. Bacteria there feed on the dead whale. Later, bacteria are eaten by small plankton, which are eaten by larger plankton, which are eaten by fish, and eventually by people. But if too many whales are killed by people and taken from the sea, living things from the ocean floor to the top of the food web are threatened.

A diver examines salmon on a fish farm in British Columbia, Canada.

Scientists are looking for ways to explore and protect marine biodiversity. Their work includes identifying as many species as possible and learning more about them. In addition, many nations have banded together to limit some fishing catches. By limiting the krill, whales, and certain other marine creatures caught each year, they help to make sure that there will be enough of each species to reproduce and survive. Fish farms in many countries are adding to the world's fish supply by spawning and raising large numbers of fish and shellfish. And every year, thousands of people from dozens of countries join in the International Coastal Clean-up to help keep the ocean waters healthy for all marine life.

All ocean life is part of a giant food web, *left*. Bacteria nourish the plankton that small and large ocean creatures feed on. Larger fish and whales feed on smaller creatures. And dead whales and other animals provide food for bacteria and certain other marine life.

ALIEN SPECIES ON BOARD

Hop aboard! But don't forget your ticket. Skippers can't be too careful these days. You see, some tiny passengers—sometimes called *aliens*—stow away on ships and cause big trouble when they reach new waters.

An alien species is one that is placed in a new location that does not have natural predators to keep its population under control. In many cases, alien species travel in a ship's *ballast water*, water that keeps the ship steady. When a ship arrives at its destination, it lets out the ballast water and any plants, animals, and other organisms in it. These alien species compete with native plants and animals for food or space.

Some of the most deadly alien arrivals are one-celled algae. In some parts of the ocean, harmful "red tides" occur when a toxic kind of *dinoflagellate* (DIH nuh FLAJ uh layt) finds itself a perfect place to "bloom," or multiply. In water containing fertilizer or sewage runoff from the land, these dinoflagellates bloom rapidly. When fish and shellfish eat the poisonous dinoflagellates, their flesh becomes poisonous to the human beings who eat them. If a bloom

This huge red tide formed about a mile off the southern California coast. The red tide stretched more than 20 miles (32 kilometers).

occurs in a smaller area, such as a bay, it can use up so much of the oxygen in the water at night that other plants and animals there may die.

To get rid of hitchhiking aliens, many freighters discharge the ballast from their holds in waters farther away from fragile parts of the ocean's system.

WILL YOU HELP THE OCEAN?

Adopt-a-Beach and other programs give volunteers a chance to help clean up beaches and shorelines.

The Pitcairn Islands in the Pacific Ocean are 3,000 miles (4,800 kilometers) from the nearest continent. Yet in 1991 more than 950 pieces of litter—bottles, plastic, toys, beer kegs, pens, medicines, and food—were found lying along one of its beaches.

Garbage is an oceanwide problem for all of us—and for you, too. Now it's clean-up time!

- Volunteer to clean up a beach or a riverbank.
- Join a marine conservation group, or start one at school.

- Recycle plastic—don't leave it on a beach or throw it overboard when boating. A hungry whale or turtle can mistake a stray milk jug or plastic bag for a meal, and then become sick.

- When you shop, look for biodegradable products, and items with a minimum of plastic packaging, so less may end up at sea.

- Help out twice a month at an oceanarium or an aquarium.

- If you see harmful chemicals, such as motor oil, antifreeze, or paint, going down a storm drain or into the ground, tell a grown-up. These chemicals need to be disposed of properly so that they don't end up in the ocean.

- Keep learning more about the ocean and ocean life so you can tell your parents and friends about how to care for the ocean, too.

What's in a tide pool? Studying one will help these students learn more about ocean life.

FIND OUT MORE

There are so many fine books and CD-ROM's about the ocean, you're sure to find plenty to enjoy. The ones listed here are only a sampling. Your school or public library will have many more.

Ages 5-8

Corals: The Sea's Great Builders
by the Cousteau Society
(Simon and Schuster Books for Young Readers, 1992)
Follow the divers of the Cousteau Society as they explore the Great Barrier Reef in Australia.

Down in the Sea: The Sea Slug
by Patricia Kite
(Albert Whitman and Co., 1994)
Have you ever seen a beautiful slug? This book is full of them! Learn how they live in the world's oceans. This book includes vivid, full-page photographs.

Fish
by Joy Richardson
(Franklin Watts, 1993)
Do fish sleep? Find out the answer to this and many of your other fish questions in this book.

The Humpback Whale
by Carol Greene
(Enslow Publishers, Inc., 1993)
Follow a humpback whale named Patch. Find out how she looks for food, hangs out with other whales, and avoids the dangers of the ocean.

The Magic School Bus on the Ocean Floor
by Joanna Cole (Scholastic, 1992)
This fictional story about a wacky class field trip that ends up in the ocean is full of facts about the water world and the creatures that live there.

The Manatee
by Carol Greene
(Enslow Publishers, Inc., 1993)
The manatee is an endangered animal. Find out how they live, and how you can help keep them alive.

Mollusks
by Joy Richardson
(Franklin Watts, 1993)
The mollusk family includes snails, oysters, and octopuses. Learn all about them in this book, which includes full-page photographs.

Sponges are Skeletons
by Barbara Juster Esbensen
(HarperCollins, 1993)
Do you know where your bath sponge came from? Do you know what it's made of? This book gives you all of the answers along with fun illustrations.

Undersea Adventure
on CD-ROM for Dos/Mac/Windows
(Knowledge Adventure, 1993)
People of all ages will learn about undersea life, including how animals live, what they eat, and how fast they swim. More than 130 organisms are described.

Ages 9 and Up

The Horseshoe Crab
by Nancy Day (Dillon Press, 1992)
Horseshoe crabs have been around for over 150 million years—and they haven't changed a bit! This book will tell you their secrets of survival.

Lobsters: Gangsters of the Sea
by Mary M. Cerullo
(Cobblehill Books, 1994)
Baby lobsters float near the surface of the water for the first few months of life. Find out how and why in this book.

Monsters of the Deep
by Norman Barrett
(Franklin Watts, 1991)
This book talks about how and where different sea animals live. It includes colorful, full-page photographs.

Sea Jellies: Rainbows in the Sea
by Elizabeth Tayntor Gowell
(Franklin Watts, 1993)
This book will tell you all about the mysterious world of the jellyfish. Find out how they swim and eat, and why they sting.

Seals, Sea Lions, and Walruses
by Victoria Sherrow
(Franklin Watts, 1991)
These three animals are all called pinnipeds. This book talks about their lives, and how you can help protect them from extinction.

The Search for the Right Whale
by Scott Kraus and Kenneth Mallory
(Crown Publishers, 1993)
In the 1980's, scientists thought that the right whale was in danger of extinction. Follow along and read about the exciting discovery of new right whale mothers and their calves.

Tentacles: The Amazing World of Octopus, Squid, and Their Relatives
by James Martin
(Crown Publishers, 1993)
When an octopus is frightened, its skin turns bright red! Find out why in this book.

Those Amazing Eels
by Cheryl M. Halton
(Dillon Press, 1990)
This book will tell you everything you need to know about eels–even how to cook them!

Watch Out for Sharks!
by Caroline Arnold
(Clarion Books, 1991)
This book follows an exhibit at the Natural History Museum of Los Angeles County. It'll tell you how different kinds of sharks live, and how to help protect them from their fiercest enemy—us!

New Words

Here are some words you have read in this book. Some may be new to you. You can see how to say them in the parentheses after the word: **aquaculture** (AHK wuh KUHL chuhr). Say the parts in small letters in your normal voice, those in small capital letters a little louder, and those in large capital letters loudest. Following the pronunciation are one or two sentences that tell the word's meaning as it is used in this book.

abyssal plain (uh BIHS uhl playn) The vast plain that covers most of the deep ocean bottom.

abyssal zone (uh BIHS uhl zohn) The layer of the deep ocean that extends from about 13,100 feet to about 19,700 feet (4,000 to 6,000 meters).

algae (AL jee) Kinds of living things in the ocean or on rocky shores that make their own food. Kelp and other seaweeds are algae. Plural of *alga*.

aquaculture (AHK wuh KUHL chuhr) The farming industry that grows algae, fish, and other sea life in the ocean.

atoll (AT ohl) A ring-shaped island formed when a coral reef grows around a volcano, which then sinks into the sea. The water enclosed by the atoll is called a **lagoon** (luh GOON).

bathyal zone (BATH ee yuhl zohn) The layer of the deep ocean that extends from about 3,300 feet to about 13,100 feet (1,000 to 4,000 meters).

biodiversity (BY oh duh VEHR suh tee) The variety of living things in a community, such as the ocean, or an area of the ocean. The greater the number of living things in a community, the greater the biodiversity of that community and the greater its chances for survival.

bioluminescence (BY oh LOO muh NEHS uhns) The ability of some living things to produce light by means of a chemical called **luciferin** (loo SIHF ur ihn), without producing heat.

bore (bawr) A high wall of churning water created by a tide that is forced into a narrow space or inlet.

chemosynthesis (KEE moh SIHN thuh sihs) The process of making food without light. Bacteria around hydrothermal vents on the ocean floor use chemosynthesis to make food with sulfur.

continental shelf (KAHN tuh NEHN tuhl shehlf) Land that gently slopes down from the edges of continents under the ocean.

crest (krehst) The highest point of a wave.

dinoflagellate (DIH nuh FLAJ uh layt) Any one of a group of one-celled algae. Some dinoflagellates are toxic and can cause harmful red tides when they multiply.

floe (floh) A huge sheet of floating ice.

food web (food wehb) The feeding pattern by which larger animals feed on smaller animals, plants, and other organisms. Tiny living things called plankton are the first source of food in the ocean food web.

greenhouse effect (GREEN hows uh FEKT) The trapping of the sun's heat near the earth; it is largely caused by gases released from automobiles, factories, and furnaces.

hadal zone (HAY duhl zohn) The deepest part of the ocean, in trenches from about 19,700 feet to more than 36,000 feet (6,000 to 11,000 meters) deep.

hydrothermal vent (HY druh THUR muhl vehnt) A jet of heated water rising from a tubelike structure in the ocean floor. A vent is created when ocean water enters cracks in newly formed rock, becomes heated, and dissolves minerals in the rock.

nekton (NEHK tuhn) Ocean animals that swim strongly enough to move independently instead of drifting with the currents.

ooze (ooz) The cover of plankton skeletons on the ocean floor.

period (PIHR ee uhd) The distance from the highest point, or crest, of one wave to the crest of the next.

phytoplankton (FY toh PLANGK tuhn) Plankton that make their own food by using energy from the sun, as plants on land do.

plankton (PLANGK tuhn) Extremely small organisms in ocean water—such as bacteria, algae, tiny animals, eggs, and larvae—that are the food source for larger animals. Masses of plankton drift with ocean currents.

polynya (puh LIHN yuh) An area of open water surrounded by sea ice and found in the same region year after year.

sediment (SEHD uh muhnt) Sand, dirt, and wastes carried by rivers into the ocean.

subduction zone (suhb DUHK shuhn zohn) An underwater area in which one part of the ocean floor pushes under a continent or another part of the ocean floor, forming deep ocean trenches and volcanoes.

submersible (suhb MUR suh buhl) An underwater vehicle that can go much deeper than a submarine, safely carrying explorers to the deepest parts of the ocean.

sunlit zone (SUHN liht zohn) The layer of ocean water extending from the surface to about as far down as sunlight reaches. The sunlit zone is full of living things.

thermocline (THUR muh klyn) A layer of ocean water that separates warm surface waters from colder, deeper waters. The temperature and density of the water change quickly in the thermocline.

trough (trawf) The lowest point of a wave; it is found in the water between the crest of two waves.

tsunami (tsoo NAH mee) A huge, powerful wave created far out at sea by an underwater earthquake or by a violent storm.

twilight zone (TWY lyt zohn) The layer of ocean water that extends from the bottom of the sunlit zone to about 3,300 feet (1,000 meters). The twilight zone is dimmer and colder and has a smaller food supply than the sunlit zone.

upwelling (uhp WEHL ihng) The rising of cold, nutrient-rich water to the surface to replace warmer water moved by wind.

wave train (wayv trayn) A group of large, powerful, smooth waves called swells that travel together across the open ocean.

zooplankton (ZOH uh PLANGK tuhn) The part of plankton made up of tiny animals that feed on phytoplankton and other small living things.

Illustration Acknowledgments

The publishers of *Childcraft* gratefully acknowledge the courtesy of the following illustrators (represented by Bernard Thornton Artists, London, except where noted), photographers, agencies, and organizations for illustrations in this volume. When all the illustrations for a sequence of pages are from a single source, the inclusive page numbers are given. Credits should be read from left to right, top to bottom, on their respective pages. All illustrations are the exclusive property of the publishers of *Childcraft* unless names are marked with an asterisk (*).

Cover: Aristocrat, Standard, and Discovery Bindings—Kristen Kest, HK Portfolio

Heritage Binding—Painting by Ken Marschall from *The Discovery of the Titanic* by Robert Ballard*; Lawrie Taylor; Tony Gibbons; Stuart Lafford; David Hall, Photo Researchers*; Tony Gibbons; Norbert Wu*; Kristen Kest, HK Portfolio; Terry Hadler

1 Lawrie Taylor
2-3 Tony Gibbons
5-7 Japack, Leo de Wys, Inc.*; Lawrie Taylor
9 Lawrie Taylor
10-11 Norbert Wu*; Lawrie Taylor
12-15 Lawrie Taylor
16-17 Terry Hadler; Lawrie Taylor
18-19 Lawrie Taylor; Terry Hadler
20-21 Terry Hadler; Lawrie Taylor
22-23 Terry Hadler; Patti Murray, Animals Animals*
24-25 Lawrie Taylor
26-27 Terry Hadler
28-31 Lawrie Taylor
32-33 Terry Hadler; Ciboux, Gamma/Liaison*
34-35 Lawrie Taylor; Natalie Fobes, Tony Stone Images*; Lawrie Taylor
36-37 Lawrie Taylor; Mathew Boysons, Panos Pictures*
38-39 John Bennett
40-41 Brandon Cole/Mo Yung Productions from Norbert Wu*; Lawrie Taylor
42-43 George Fryer; Lawrie Taylor
44-45 Lawrie Taylor; Andrew J. Martinez, Photo Researchers*
46-47 Tony Gibbons; Norbert Wu*
48-49 Tony Gibbons; Robert Frerck*
50-51 Jim Zipp, Photo Researchers*; Lawrie Taylor; Zig Lesczynski, Animals Animals*
52-53 Jeff Rotman*; Gregory Ochocki, Photo Researchers*; Jeff Rotman*
54-55 Tony Gibbons; Lawrie Taylor; Terry Hadler
56-57 Tony Gibbons; Rodger Jackman/OSF from Animals Animals*; Scott Johnson, Animals Animals*
58-59 Stuart Lafford; Lawrie Taylor
60-61 Jack Dermid, Photo Researchers*; Nuridsany & Perennou, Photo Reseachers*
63 Lawrie Taylor
64-65 Tom McHugh, Photo Researchers*; Tony Gibbons; Lawrie Taylor
66-67 W. Gregory Brown, Animals Animals*; Lawrie Taylor; David Spears, Bruce Coleman, Ltd.*
68-69 Japack, Leo de Wys, Inc.*; Rick Browne, Monterey Bay Aquarium*
70-71 Malcolm Ellis; Lawrie Taylor
73 M. A. Chappell, Animals Animals*
74-75 S. J. Krasemann from Peter Arnold*; Lawrie Taylor
76-77 Andrew J. Martinez from Fred Bavendam*; Lawrie Taylor
78-79 Terry Hadler; Lawrie Taylor; Eric Hartmann, Magnum*
80-81 Tony Gibbons; D. P. Wilson/ Science Source from Photo Researchers*; Lawrie Taylor
82-83 Terry Hadler; Lawrie Taylor; Keith Gillett, Earth Scenes*; Kjell B. Sandved, Photo Researchers*
84-85 Colin Newman; Kelvin Aitken from Peter Arnold*; Jeff Rotman from Peter Arnold*
86-87 Terry Hadler; Lawrie Taylor; David Hall, Photo Researchers*
88-89 Tony Gibbons
90-91 Jeff Rotman*; Tony Gibbons; Jeff Rotman*
92-93 Lawrie Taylor; Neville Coleman, Underwater Geographic*; J. Carnemolla, Australian Picture Library*
94-95 Japack, Leo de Wys, Inc.*; Wayne Hasson*
96-97 Tony Gibbons; Jeff Rotman*; Lawrie Taylor
98-99 Tony Gibbons; Jeff Rotman*; Robert Frerck*
100-101 Norbert Wu from Peter Arnold*; Tony Gibbons
102-103 Lawrie Taylor
104-105 Lawrie Taylor; Takeshi Takahara, Photo Researchers*; Lawrie Taylor
106-107 Steven L. Waterman, Photo Researchers*; Lawrie Taylor
108-109 Bob Cranston/Mo Yung Productions from Norbert Wu*; Lawrie Taylor
110-113 Lawrie Taylor
114-115 Lawrie Taylor; Alex Abel; Jeff Rotman*; Colin Newman
116-117 Malcolm Ellis
118-119 Frans Lanting, Photo Researchers*; Lawrie Taylor
120-121 Lawrie Taylor
122-123 Lawrie Taylor; Norbert Wu*; C. Prescott-Allen, Animals Animals*
124-125 Norbert Wu*; Victoria McCormick, Animals Animals*
126-127 Japack, Leo de Wys, Inc.*; Michael Boytoff, Black Star*
128-129 Lawrie Taylor; Jeff Rotman*
130-131 Tom McHugh, Photo Researchers*; Colin Newman
132-133 Colin Newman
134-135 Lawrie Taylor; Norbert Wu*; Norbert Wu*
136-137 Tony Gibbons
138-139 Lawrie Taylor; Terry Hadler
140-141 Terry Hadler
142-143 Norbert Wu*; Lawrie Taylor
144-145 Lawrie Taylor
146 Lawrie Taylor; Norbert Wu*
148-149 Tony Gibbons
150-151 Norbert Wu*; Lawrie Taylor
152-153 Lawrie Taylor; Terry Hadler
154-155 Jack Donnelly, WHOI*; Terry Hadler
156-157 Lawrie Taylor; Al Giddings, Images Unlimited*; Natural History Photographic Agency*
158-159 Japack, Leo de Wys, Inc.*; Seth Resnick*
160-161 Bettmann Archive*; Painting by Ken Marschall from *The Discovery of the Titanic* by Robert Ballard*
163 WHOI*
164-165 Culver Pictures*; Painting by Ken Marschall from *The Discovery of the Titanic* by Robert Ballard*
166-167 Terry Hadler
168-169 Bryan & Cherry Alexander*; Lawrie Taylor
170-173 Lawrie Taylor
174-175 Lawrie Taylor; Bryan & Cherry Alexander*
176-177 Bryan & Cherry Alexander*
178-179 Tony Gibbons; Lawrie Taylor
180-181 Norbert Rosing/OSF from Animals Animals*; Bryan & Cherry Alexander*
182-183 Lawrie Taylor; David Thelwell
185 John Bennett
186-187 Lawrie Taylor; Robert Morton
188-189 Colin Newman
190-191 Harold E. Wilson, Animals Animals*; Brian Milne, Animals Animals*; Lawrie Taylor
192-193 Malcolm Ellis; John Gerlach, Animals Animals*; Bryan & Cherry Alexander*
194 Malcolm Ellis
195-199 Lawrie Taylor
200-201 Japack, Leo de Wys, Inc.*; Bryan & Cherry Alexander*
202-203 NASA*; Lawrie Taylor
204 Lawrie Taylor; Tony Gibbons
206-207 Tony Gibbons
208-209 Tony Gibbons; Natalie Fobes, Tony Stone Images*
210-211 Lawrie Taylor; Peter Franks, University of California, San Diego*
212-213 Lawrie Taylor; David Young-Wolff, PhotoEdit*; Brandon Cole/Mo Yung Productions from Norbert Wu*
214-219 Lawrie Taylor

INDEX

This index is an alphabetical list of important topics covered in this book. It will help you find information given in both words and pictures. To help you understand what an entry means, there is sometimes a helping word in parentheses, for example, **alligator** (animal). If there is information in both words and pictures, you will see the words *with pictures* in parentheses after the page number. If there is only a picture, you will see the word *picture* in parentheses after the page number.

abyssal plain, 145 *(with picture)*
abyssal zone, 144 *(with picture)*
albatross (bird), 116, 117
algae (seaweed), 34-35, 46, 47, 210
alien species, 210-211
alligator (animal), 49, 61
Alvin (submersible), 162, 165 *(picture)*
ama diver (occupation), 104 *(with picture)*
anglerfish, 147 *(with picture)*
Angus (machine), 162
Antarctic (region), 169-173 *(with pictures)*
  animals of, 186-189 *(with pictures),* 191-194 *(with pictures)*
  climate of, 196, 199
  ozone hole over, 200-201
  polynyas in, 183
Antarctica (continent) ice of, 171-173 *(with pictures),* 197
  pollution in, 201
  study of, 200-201 *(with picture)*
Antarctic Ocean, 12
  animals in, 186-189 *(with pictures)*
  ice covering, 171
  ridge through, 141 *(with picture)*
aquaculture (farming), 34-35
  see also **farming**
archerfish, 61
Arctic (region), 169-173 *(with pictures)*
  animals of, 178-184 *(with pictures),* 190-194 *(with pictures)*
  climate of, 199
  ice of, 174-177 *(with pictures)*
Arctic Ocean, 12, 37, 170-173 *(with pictures)*
  animals in, 178-181 *(with picture)*
  continental shelf in, 78
  polynyas in, 182-184 *(with picture)*
  ridge through, 141 *(with picture)*
Argo (machine), 161-162
Ascension Island (Atlantic Ocean), 123
Atlantic Ocean, 12
  coral reefs in, 85
  green turtle migration to, 122, 125
  Gulf Stream in, 27 *(picture)*
  ridge through, 141 *(with picture)*
  Titanic disaster in, 160
atoll (reef), 86 *(with picture)*
Australia, Great Barrier Reef of, 18 *(with picture),* 82-86 *(with pictures)*

bacteria (organisms), 154, 209
Bahía Paraíso (ship), 201
Ballard, Robert (scientist), 154 *(picture),* 160-165
ballast water, 210-211
barnacle (animal), 46, 50 *(picture),* 61
barrier reef, 86 *(with picture),* 92
bathyal zone, 144 *(with picture)*
Bay of Fundy (Canada), 21
beach, 18
  garbage on, 212-213
  life on, 43, 47-48 *(with picture),* 54-57
  see also **seashore**
bear, polar, 179-180 *(with pictures)*
beluga (whale), 180-181 *(with picture),* 183
Benguela Current, 28
biodiversity, 206-209
bioluminescence (light), 134-135 *(with picture),* 147, 149, 150
bird
  open ocean, 18, 115-118 *(with pictures)*
  polar regions, 183 *(with picture),* 190-194 *(with pictures)*
  seashore, 70-75 *(with pictures)*
  see also names of individual birds
black smoker, *see* **hydrothermal vent**
blade, of kelp, 96 *(with picture)*
blubber (fat), 180
booby (bird), 121
bore (water), 22
buoyancy compensator (clothing), 105 *(with picture)*

Canada, Bay of Fundy in, 21
canyon, 16 *(with picture)*
Carson, Rachel (biologist), 79 *(with picture)*
Challenger Deep (region), 156
chemosynthesis (process), 154
chitin (material), 36
clam (animal), 35-36, 69
  giant, 157 *(picture)*
  razor, 48 *(with picture)*
climate, 195-201 *(with pictures)*
  see also **weather**
cloud, 24-25
clownfish, 89 *(with picture)*
comb jelly (animal), 135 *(with picture)*
continental margin (region), 78 *(with picture)*
continental rise (region), 78 *(with picture)*
continental shelf (region), 16, 78 *(with pictures),* 79
continental slope (region), 78 *(with picture)*
continents, movement of, 138-140

copepod (animal), 135
coral (animal), 82-85 *(with pictures)*
cabbage, 84 *(picture)*
see also **coral reef**
coralline (algae), 47
coral polyp (animal), 84-85 *(with pictures)*
coral reef, 18 *(with picture),* 82-93 *(with pictures)*
cordgrass, 48
crab (animal), 47, 49, 72, 152, 187
fiddler, 60-61 *(with picture)*
hermit, 41, 51 *(picture),* 98
kelp, 99 *(with picture)*
pea, 47
porcelain, 53
spider, 91 *(picture)*
crest, of wave, 20 *(with picture)*
current (water), 26-28 *(with picture)*
energy from, 37
ice flows from, 176
life in, 110 *(with picture)*
origin of, 185
polynyas and, 184
seashore and, 42, 43
wastes washed away by, 205-206

day, length of, 21
Dead Sea, 15
Deep, the (region), 143-145 *(with pictures)*
exploration of, 158-159
hydrothermal vents in, 152-155 *(with picture)*
life in, 146-150 *(with pictures),* 152, 154-156 *(with pictures)*
Titanic wreck in, 160-165 *(with pictures)*
Deep Flight (submersible), 159
demand regulator (machine), 104
de Vernal, Anne (scientist), 198, 199
dinoflagellate (organism), 210-211 *(with picture)*
diving, 103-106 *(with pictures)*
by ama divers, 104 *(with picture)*
by birds, 121
in submersibles, 158-159
scuba, 104-105
surface-supplied, 106 *(with picture)*
dolphin (animal), 18 *(with picture),* 109, 115
dangers to, 126-127 (with picture)
swimming by, 120
Domack, Eugene, 198
dovekie (bird), 191
dragonfish, 150 *(with picture)*
drift net, 126
duck, eider (bird), 184, 190 *(with picture)*

Earle, Sylvia (scientist), 158-159 *(with picture)*
earthquake, 22 *(with picture)*
eel (fish)
gulper, 148 *(with picture)*
moray, 90-91 *(with picture)*
eelpout (fish), 152
egg
Arctic birds, 190 *(with picture),* 192-194 *(with picture)*
fish, 179, 187
green turtle, 122-123 *(with picture)*
El Niño (weather), 30-33 *(with pictures)*
energy, from ocean, 37
ENSO cycle, 30
environmental issues
fishing, *see* **fishing**
global warming, 197-199
hunting, 180, 209
ozone hole, 200-201
pollution, *see* **pollution**

face mask (diving equipment), 103, 104 *(picture)*
fairy basselet (fish), 87 *(with picture)*
farming
of fish, 34-35, 209 *(with picture)*
of kelp, 101
fish
coral reef, 87-92 *(with pictures)*
deep-ocean, 146-150 *(with pictures)*
farming of, 34-35, 209 *(with picture)*
food for, 80, 112
kelp forest, 99-100
mangrove forest, 61 *(with pictures)*
open ocean, 114-115 *(with pictures)*
polar regions, 178-179 *(with pictures),* 187 *(with picture)*
scale-dating, 119 *(with picture)*
see also **fishing** *and names of individual fish*
fishing
dolphins caught in, 126-127
El Niño and, 32
endangering ocean, 204-205, 209
for sea cucumbers, 94-95 *(with picture)*
flamingo (bird), 49 *(picture)*
flipper (diving equipment), 103 *(with picture)*
flying, water, 121
food, from ocean, 34-35, 94-95
food web, 80, 90, 209 *(with picture)*
forest, 92, 204
kelp, 96-101 *(with pictures),* 204
mangrove, 58-62 *(with pictures)*
France, Rance River Dam in, 37 *(with picture)*
fringing reef, 86 *(with picture)*
frond (part of seaweed), 46
furniture polish, 100

Galapagos Islands (Pacific Ocean), 94-95
gannet (bird), 117, 121
garbage, *see* **pollution**
geomagnetic sense, 125
geophysics (science), 200
glaciologist (scientist), 200
glasswort (plant), 48
global warming, 197-199, 205
goby (fish), 53, 90
Godzilla (hydrothermal vent), 153
grass, 48
grease (ice), 174
Great Barrier Reef (Australia), 18 *(with picture),* 82-86 *(with pictures)*
Great Meteor (mountain), 141
greenhouse effect, 197 *(with picture),* 199
Greenland (island), 170, 172, 184
grouper (fish), 87 *(with picture)*
grunt (fish), 87

Gulf of Mexico, 37
Gulf Stream, 26-27 *(with picture)*
gull (bird), 23 *(picture),* 72, 116
black-headed, 72
herring, 70 *(picture),* 72
ivory, 182 *(picture)*
ring-billed, 70 *(picture)*

hadal zone, 144 *(with picture),* 156
hatchet fish, 148-149
holdfast (part of seaweed), 44, 97-98 *(with picture)*
hot vent, *see* **hydrothermal vent**
Humboldt Current, 28
hummock (ridge), 176 *(with picture)*
hunting, 180, 184, 209
hydrothermal vent, 19 *(with picture),* 151 *(with pictures),* 152-155 *(with picture),* 162

ice, 170-172, 174-177 *(with pictures)*
blue, 175
candle, 174
first-year, 174
melting in polar regions, 196-199
multiyear, 174-175
pack or fast, 174-176, 178
pancake, 174-175 *(with picture)*
polynyas and, 182
slob, 174
young, 177
iceberg, 172 *(with picture),* 196-197
icecap, 19, 171, 197
ice cream, 100
icefish, 187 *(with picture)*
ice floe, 176 *(with picture),* 177
imprinting (behavior), 124
Indian Ocean, 12, 30, 85, 141 *(with picture)*
insect, 46
International Coastal Clean-up (conservation), 209
International Geophysical Year (study), 200-201
Inuit (people), 173, 183, 184, 191
island, 86 *(with picture),* 141

Japan, ama divers of, 104 *(with picture)*
Jason Junior (robot), 162, 164
jellyfish (animal), 150
Jules's Undersea Lodge (Florida), 17

kelp (seaweed)
as food, 34-35, 206
forests of, 96-101 *(with pictures),* 204
on seashore, 44
kombu (food), 34
krill (animal), 173, 186 *(with picture),* 188, 209
Kuroshio Current, 28

lagoon, 86 *(with picture)*
La Niña (weather), 30
lanternfish, 135 *(with picture),* 143 *(with picture),* 149-150
lead (ice), 177
lichen, sea, *see* **sea lichen**
life, origin of, 155
limpet (animal), 46 *(with picture)*
luciferin (enzyme), 135
lugworm (animal), 55 *(with pictures)*

mackerel (fish), 114
magma (molten rock), 138-139 *(with picture)*
magnetite (mineral), 125
manganese (mineral), 36
mangrove (tree), 58-62 *(with pictures),* 92
Marine Mammal Stranding Center (New Jersey), 127
marlin (fish), 114
medicine, from ocean, 35-36
Mediterranean Sea, 15 *(with picture),* 21
meteorologist (scientist), 200
Mid-Ocean Ridge, 141 *(with picture)*
migration, by green turtles, 122-125 *(with pictures)*
mile, nautical, 15
minerals, from ocean, 36-37
mining, of ocean, 36-37
mollusk (animal), 44-46 *(with pictures),* 187
Monterey Bay Aquarium (California), 68
mountain, in ocean, 16 *(with picture),* 138-141 *(with pictures)*
mudskipper (fish), 61-62 *(with picture)*
murre (bird), 190 *(with picture)*
mussel (animal), 35, 53, 61

natural gas, 37
nautical mile, 15
nekton (animals), 81
North Pole, 19, 27, 170, 197
North Sea, 37
North Water Polynya (water), 182-184 *(with picture)*
nudibranch (animal), 52 *(with picture)*

ocean
depth of, 13, 156
sea and, 15
size of, 12
temperature of, 14
ocean floor, 17 *(with picture)*
Antarctic region, 187
spreading of, 138-141 *(with pictures)*
oceanographer (scientist), 11
Ocean Thermal Energy Conversion, 37
octopus (animal), 76
oil
from ocean, 37
spilled by ship, 201
ooze (material), 145
orca (whale), 188, 194
oscillation (movement), 30
OTEC (power), 37
otter, *see* **sea otter**
oyster (animal), 34, 61, 74
oystercatcher (bird), 70 *(picture),* 74
ozone layer, 200-201

Pacific Ocean, 12
continental shelf in, 78
coral reefs in, 85, 86
El Niño and, 30-32
Galapagos Islands in, 94-95
hydrothermal vents in, 152
pollution in, 212
ridge through, 141 *(with picture)*
parrotfish, 88

pelican (bird), 71-72
(with picture)
penguin (bird), 28, 186, 192
(with picture)
Adélie, 192 *(with picture),*
194 *(picture)*
chinstrap, 192
emperor, 192-193
gentoo, 192 *(with picture)*
king, 192
pepiñero (fisherman), 94-95
(with picture)
period, of wave, 21 *(with picture)*
periwinkle (animal), 46 *(with*
picture)
Persian Gulf, 37
petrel (bird), 116, 117, 121
phytoplankton (organisms),
81, 178
Pitcairn Islands (Pacific Ocean),
212
plankton (organisms)
as food, 80-81 *(with picture),*
114 *(with picture),* 149, 209
in Arctic, 178, 179
plastic, as pollution, 213
Pliny (naturalist), 35
plover (bird)
crab, 72
semi-palmated, 71 *(picture)*
poles, of Earth, *see* **North Pole;**
South pole
pollution
air, 197, 201
alien species, 210-211
birds and, 72, 75
danger to ocean from,
205-209 *(with picture)*
dolphins and, 126-127
garbage on beaches,
212-213
in polar regions, 180, 201
in reefs, 93
polynya (water), 182-184 *(with*
picture)
polyp, coral, *see* **coral polyp**
proboscis (body part), 52
puffin (bird), 116-117 *(with*
picture)
tufted, 190
pup (young)
of sea otter, 68-69
(with picture)
of shark, 130, 133
pycnogonid (animal), *see*
sea spider

ragworm (animal), 56 *(with*
picture)
rain
El Niño and, 30-33
in water cycle, 25
waves and, 29 *(with picture)*
Rance River (France), 37 *(with*
picture)
red tide (pollution), 210-211
(with picture)
reef, coral, *see* **coral reef**
remora (fish), 132 *(with picture)*
ribbonfish, 135-136
Riftia (worm), 155 *(with picture)*
river, 43, 48
rockweed (seaweed), 44 *(picture)*
"rusticle," 163 *(with picture)*

sailfish, 114, 120
sailor (occupation), 38-39
salmon (fish), 34 *(with picture),*
209 *(picture)*
salp (animal), 135
salt
arctic tern and, 192
in ice, 174
in ocean, 13
mangroves and, 59
salt marsh, 48-49 *(with picture)*
sand, on beach, 47-48, 54-57
sanderling (bird), 73 *(with picture)*
sandpiper (bird), 73
scallop, queen (animal), 65-66
(with picture)
Schoelkopf, Bob
(conservationist), 127
scuba diving, 104-105
sculpin (fish), 178 *(with picture)*
sea, 15
sea anemone (animal), 35
in Antarctic, 187 *(with picture)*
in coral reefs, 88-90
(with picture)
in ocean trenches, 156
in tide pools, 50-52
(with picture)
seabed viewer, 63 *(with picture)*
sea blite (plant), 48
sea butterfly (animal), 179
sea cucumber (animal), 94-95
(with picture)
sea gooseberry (animal), 179
sea gull (bird), *see* **gull**
seal (animal), 169 *(with picture),*
173, 183, 186, 189
crabeater, 189
hunted by polar bear, 180
Weddell, 189 *(with picture)*
sea lavender (plant), 48
sea level, 197-199
sea lichen (plant), 46
seamount (mountain), 141
sea mouse (animal), 57 *(with*
picture)
sea otter (animal), 100 *(with*
picture)
California, 68-69 *(with picture)*
sea parrot, *see* **puffin**
seashore, 17, 42-49 *(with pictures)*
life in waters near, 64-74
(with pictures)
tide pools on, 50-53
(with pictures)
see also **beach**
sea spider (animal), 19, 50-52,
156 *(with picture),* 188
sea star, *see* **starfish**
sea urchin (animal), 47
Sea Watchers (group), 62
seaweed, 34
forests of, 96-101 *(with pictures)*
near shore, 44-47 *(with pictures)*
see also **kelp**
sea worm, *see* **worm**
sediment, 43
seed, movement of, 48, 120
shark, sand tiger (fish), 128-
133 *(with pictures)*
sheathbill (bird), 194
shell
of deep-ocean creatures, 156
of mollusk, 44-46 *(with pictures)*
of oyster, 74
of scallop, 65-66 *(with pictures)*
ship
ballast water discharged from,
210-211
oil spill from, 201
see also **submersible**
shipwreck, 27
Titanic, 160-165 *(with pictures)*
shore, of ocean, *see* **seashore**
shrimp (animal), 90, 150, 179
in twilight zone, 135, 136
pistol, 67 *(with picture)*

siphonophore (animal), 152
skua (bird), 194 *(with picture)*
slug (animal), 52 *(with picture)*
snail (animal), 46 *(with picture)*, 99
snailfish, 178-179 *(with picture)*
snorkeling, 105 *(with picture)*
snow, 25, 171, 198-199
"snow" (food), 112
Southern Ocean, *see* **Antarctic Ocean**
South Pole, 19, 171, 197
Spain, and treasure hunting, 27
sponge (animal), 35, 47, 187
spoonbill (bird), 74 *(with picture)*
squid (animal), 137, 150
giant, 136 *(with picture)*, 137
starfish (animal), 47, 50 *(picture)*
bat star, 98 *(with picture)*
brittle star, 98 *(with picture)*, 150, 187 *(with picture)*
crown-of-thorns, 90-91 *(with picture)*
stargazer (fish), 67 *(with picture)*
stipe (part of organism), 96 *(picture)*, 99 *(with picture)*
subduction zone, 139 *(picture)*, 140
submersible (vehicle), 145, 158, 159, 162
sunlit zone, 110-112 *(with pictures)*
swamp (area), 205
swim bladder (organ), 147
swimming, by sea animals, 120
swordfish, 114 *(with picture)*, 120, 202
symbiosis (process), 90

teeth, of shark, 128 *(picture)*, 130 *(with picture)*
temperature
ocean water, 14
on Earth, *see* **climate**
tern (bird), 117-118
Arctic, 191-192 *(with picture)*
least, 70 *(picture)*
territorial rights, over ocean, 15
tether (diving equipment), 158-159
thermal energy, 37
thermocline (water), 30-32 *(with pictures)*, 113 *(with picture)*
tide, 59
energy from, 37 *(with picture)*
seashore and, 42-43 *(with pictures)*
tide pools and, 50
waves from, 21-22
tide pool, 50-53 *(with pictures)*, 213 *(picture)*
Titanic (ship), 160-165 *(with pictures)*
toothpaste, 100
topsnail (animal), 99
treasure hunting, 27
trench, ocean, 139 *(picture)*, 140, 156 *(with picture)*
trepang (food), 94
tropicbird, 118 *(with picture)*
trough, of wave, 20 *(with picture)*
tsunami (wave), 22-23 *(with picture)*
tub gurnard (fish), 64-65 *(with picture)*
tuna (fish), 114 *(with picture)*, 120, 126
turnstone, ruddy (bird), 70 *(picture)*
turtle, green (animal), 122-125 *(with pictures)*
twilight zone, 110-112 *(with pictures)*, 134-137 *(with pictures)*

upwelling (water), 26, 184

Vailoces, Wilson (farmer), 62
viperfish, 134 *(picture)*, 136
volcano, 86 *(with picture)*, 138-141 *(with picture)*

wahoo (fish), 114
walrus (animal), 177 *(with picture)*, 183 *(with picture)*
water cycle, 24-25
water pressure, 14, 107 *(with picture)*
waves, 20-23 *(with pictures)*
ice flows from, 176
rain and, 29 *(with picture)*
seashore and, 42, 43
wastes washed away by, 205-206
wave train, 23
weather, 24-28 *(with pictures)*
El Niño, 30-33 *(with pictures)*
global warming and, 197
see also **climate**
weever (fish), 66 *(with picture)*
wetland (area), 205-206 *(with picture)*
whale (animal), 115, 120, 188
beluga, 180-181 *(with picture)*, 183
caught in fishing nets, 205
in food web, 207-209 *(with picture)*
orca or killer, 188, 194
sperm, 136 *(with picture)*
whelk (animal), 53 *(with picture)*
wind
currents from, 25-26
El Niño and, 30-32
ice flows from, 176
polynyas and, 184
seashore and, 42, 43
waves from, 20-23 *(with pictures)*
worm (animal), 47, 54-57 *(with pictures)*, 150, 152
Antarctic, 187
beard, 156
peacock, 56-57 *(with picture)*
polychaete, 156
Riftia, 155 *(with picture)*
tube, 47, 154 *(picture)*
wrack (seaweed)
bladder, 47 *(with picture)*
channel, 44
spiral, 46

zooplankton (organisms), 81, 114 *(with picture)*, 178, 179, 191

Exploring the ocean.